Rent to Own Profit$ for Canadian$

How to Make BIG Money in
Rent to Own Real Estate Investing,
The "Win-Win-Win" Way!

By Dave Dubeau
& Dan Dubeau

Library and Archives Canada Cataloguing in Publication

Dubeau, Dave, 1968-
Rent to own profit$ for Canadian$: how to make big money in rent to own real estate investing, the "win-win-win" way! / by Dave Dubeau & Dan Dubeau..

ISBN 978-0-9783090-6-0

1. Real estate investment--Canada. 2. Renting to own--Canada. I. Dubeau, Dan, 1955- II. Title. III. Title: Rent to own profits for Canadians.

HD316.D82 2011 332.63'240971 C2011-902536-1

Illustrations by David Allred Studios
Cover and Graphic Design by Webgrity

April Dew Publishing
Suite 1, 504 Delmar Ave.
Pointe Claire, QC H9R 4A6

TABLE OF CONTENTS

What Canadian Real Estate Investors Are Saying About "Rent to Own Profits for Canadians"

Just finished reading your book and I must tell you that it is crammed full of very useful hands-on information for anyone interested in R20 property investing as well as being very informative for personal use. Thoroughly enjoyed it and learned a lot in the process. I am sure to keep it handy and put it to use in my future real estate investing. A great resource. Thanks again for all the information.

Joanne Gervais

...you are selling the book title short by just focusing it on rent to own! In fact, quite a bit of this book goes into the psychology of why [investing in] real estate over, say, mutual funds or other investments –. into what you need to do after you purchase your property, and very comprehensive steps to maintaining, and exit strategies after. Expand your title – it's a great book. Again, THANK YOU and thank you for allow me... the pleasure of reviewing it.

Kathy Long, professional real estate investor
Sherwood Park, AB

Reading Rent to Own Profit$" has opened my mind to all kinds of creative ways to structure real estate deals. Dave goes through many different scenarios and shows how each strategy can benefit specific situations. This book has changed the way I do business!"

Jon Simcoe
Fort McMurray, AB

I thought your book had a ton of useful information. It is straightforward and a quick read. I am completely new to the idea of R2O, and I found reading this was a good way to learn. I have a much better understanding of the process and opportunity involved. I also appreciated the many tips that are not only useful for R2O, but also transferrable to any real estate business such as what to look for in a team and useful marketing tools.

Randy Maus
Calgary, AB

It is easy to read, practical and straight forward. Best for any level of real estate investor. Highly recommended!!!

Jet Y. Chu

I have just finished reading this book after quite a few weeks, and I must say, it has given me a much better insight on the Rent to Own business! It is a well written, thorough, and very easy to understand book that is full of information to prepare investors of what is to come. Rent to Own: Profits for Canadians explains developing a business plan, attracting clients, screening potential tenants, right through to finalizing the sale and handing over the keys. I am eager to involve myself in the various types of Rent to Own strategies and potentially begin my own Rent to Own company using the methods and skills that I have learnt in this book. Thanks Dave and Dan Dubeau for explaining R2O so well!

Glenn Mapp

INTRODUCTION

The title of this book is Rent-to-Own Profits for Canadians, How to Make BIG Money in Rent-to-Own Real Estate Investing the Win-Win-Win Way. In a nutshell, its intention is to help you, the reader, to learn everything you need to do to complete your very first Rent-to-Own (R2O) real estate deal.

By making use of the information provided in this book – expert guidance about R2Os – you will help a deserving family achieve the dream of owning a starter home much quicker than they would otherwise be able to. How are we going to do that? We'll take you by the hand and show you the ropes, so you know exactly how the business works.

Before we start, however, we want to congratulate you for purchasing this book. You've made a very wise investment decision, especially if you're ready to take control of your own finances and jump into real estate investing in a serious way.

Why R2O? In our opinion, the Rent-to-Own method is the best way to invest in real estate. It allows you to create significant monthly cash flow income for the least number of problems in terms of management, as well as for many other reasons, which we'll get into in more detail as we go through the book.

Now, there are other books on Rent-to-Own real estate investing. For example, Investing in Rent-to-Own Property by Mark Loeffler is a really good book, which we highly recommend.

We're writing our own book because we've got a slightly different perspective. We're not saying that one's right and the other's wrong. They're just different, and we want to explain our view on Rent-to-Own real estate investing. We think it's good for people to have multiple perspectives.

A good thing about R2Os is that this model gives you, the investor, peace of mind. You can't put a price on that, especially in today's volatile market.

As an example, when we purchase a Rent-to-Own property, it is in essence pre-sold. We have an exit strategy in place. We're not worried about fluctuations in the real estate market, the stock market or interest rates. We have put a well-qualified person in that home, and the intention is for that person to enjoy the house and purchase it from us within a couple of years at a predetermined price. So, we have that peace of mind and some back-up provisions to protect us in case we have to revert to a plan B or a plan C as alternative exit strategies if things don't work out. That's a huge relief. R2O offers you much more control over your money than stocks, bonds or mutual funds – all of which can be wiped away, practically overnight, in a recession.

With the Rent-to-Own option, you will know what to expect in terms of steady returns, which are much higher than the ones generated by the stock market. You don't have to worry about volatility and uncertainty, and that in itself is worth a pot of gold. You can sleep much better knowing that your money is safe.

A beautiful thing about real estate investing with your investors is that they have a tangible asset – a chunk of dirt that they actually own, as compared to mutual funds, which is a pool of a whole bunch of different stocks and a whole bunch of different companies – basically all paper. We've seen in the past couple of years how even the most solid blue chip companies can tank, go under and be bailed out by the government. In many cases, people had to kiss their investments goodbye because they had no control over these downward forces. So at the end of the day, your investments are not even worth the price of the paper they're printed on.

When investing in real estate with your investors, you actually have properties – very tangible, very real. People need housing – it's a basic human necessity. There's no such thing on the face of this earth as an absolutely guaranteed investment, but real estate is the closest thing that we've found to it. So, that's part of the reason we like it so much.

And the biggest thing we like about the way we do our Rent-to-Own real estate investing is that it is truly a win-win-win proposition.

Your Client Wins:

By offering a R2O option, we are able to help people become homeowners much faster than they ever could on their own. That makes a huge impact on people's lives. These folks (we will refer to them as "clients" in this book) are thrilled to be able to get into a home of their own on a R2O basis. They've been turned down by the banks and by the mortgage brokers. But we're making it possible for them to get their own home, and the way we do it, they can even pick out the house! (We'll talk about that further in the book as well.)

Your Investors Win:

Our investors make a very, very good return on their money with the security of owning real estate and without having to deal with tenants and toilet hassles. Their investment time frame is much shorter than with traditional real estate investing, and they know going into the deal exactly what the exit strategy is, what their ROI (return on investment) will be, and when they are going to get paid. It is very simple and clear cut.

You Win:

Of course, as the "deal makers" ourselves, as the people putting all the pieces together, we're making very, very good profits on our R2O deals. Sums such as $20,000, $30,000, $40,000 or even more profit per deal is not uncommon. A lot of our profit comes to us in up-front fees and monthly cash flow. Whereas many "traditional" investors are thrilled to have $75 to $100 a month per door in net cash flow, with our R2O methodology, we are able to get as much as $1,000 a month in NET positive cash flow from a single property! That is the equivalent of having 10 "traditional" rental units!

Unfortunately, a lot of times, real estate investors get a bad rap, are accused of being "slumlords", and of taking advantage of unsuspecting homeowners and tenants. While it is true that there are a few unscrupulous investors out there, most of us are good people trying to offer a valuable service. We'll talk about that in future chapters.

With certain types of real estate investing, you almost have to "steal" the property in order to make money on it – get "instant equity" by buying at bargain prices. These particular folks get the reputation of preying on little old ladies, trying to take advantage of them, "stealing" their houses for under market value, and all that kind of unsavoury stuff.

That's one way of making money in real estate, but you have to have a pretty thick skin and tough personality to make a go of it. It is typically a "win-lose" proposition.

That's not how we do business with our R2Os. We are very transparent. The cards are all on the table. The fact is, you don't have to be sneaky or try to pull the wool over anybody's eyes to be successful in real estate investing. We just put it all out there, and everybody likes the deal. We'll talk a lot more about that in Chapter Two – about why we chose Rent-to-Own to invest in real estate.

In this book, we're not looking at luxury homes or multimillion-dollar properties. We will be focusing on starter, entry-level homes, which is a sector of real estate that has the least volatility.

Not everybody needs a million-dollar mansion, but there will always be a lot of people in the market for starter homes.

Clearly, if you are new to R2O investing, you will need all the guidance you can get. This is where we come in. Our goal is to help you avoid some of the hurdles that we had to go through ourselves. We had to figure out a lot of things and tweak what other people had done based on the US market. Things are different in Canada, and we're hoping to cut out the unnecessary part of the learning curve and fast-track you to our Rent-to-Own concept, so you can start using and profiting from it much faster than we were able to.

We wish a book like this would have been available when we first started!

The overall goal of this book is to help you buy at least your very first Rent-to-Own investment property. We'll take you through it step-by-step, and show you the business from A to Z: Exactly how things work here in Canada, how we do it, how we found it to be a very effective formula, and how you can too. We're going to show you some things that other people haven't talked about in other books, especially when it comes to marketing and attracting qualified clients.

The other goal is to show you the pros and cons of the business. If, after reading this book, you decide that Rent-to-Own is not the kind of business you want to be in, then at least you'll know. After all, real estate investing is not for everyone. Knowing that will save you a lot of hassle of stumbling through a deal or two, and then finding out that's not what you want to do.

Ready to start? Great, let's get into it!

We suggest that you have a pen and a highlighter handy as you're reading the book. Make sure to do what we do: Mark it up, take notes, write notes in it, and just make it your own book. The more interactive you are with it, the more you are going to get out of it.

We're looking forward to showing you how we do Rent-to-Own real estate investing right here in Canada and why we think it is such a win, win, win way of doing business.

About the Authors

Dave Dubeau

I grew up in beautiful Taylor, British Columbia, just outside of Fort St. John. I went to UBC and got a B.A. (Basically Asinine) degree in psychology. I traveled to Mexico and Central America for several years after that because, for some reason, nobody was offering me any high paying jobs in Canada. Then, I settled down in San Jose, Costa Rica, where I met my lovely wife Susy. We had our children Amy and Andrew. I owned a language training company down there for just over 10 years.

In 2003, Susy and I decided to move back to Canada. We felt it was a better option for the children, more secure. I left my business in Costa Rica and had to start from scratch in Canada. That's when I got into creative real estate investing. I took some of those late night TV "How to Get Rich in Real Estate" courses from our American friends. I had to figure out how to adapt them to our unique Canadian situation. My claim to fame is that I did 18 flips in 18 months between 2003 and 2005. Then I started working with "Canadian Rich Dad," Darren Weeks. Together, we started the Fast Track Inner Circle membership program. I quickly became the marketing director for his companies and helped grow his business from two or three employees to well over 100 today, and over $100 million a year in sales.

At our annual Christmas get-together in 2009, my big brother Dan was really keen on his real estate business. Things were starting to take off for him and he bent my ear about it. I had taken time off from real estate while I was working with Darren Weeks. But what Dan was doing was very, very interesting. He got into the Rent-to-Own (R2O) business with his own unique twist. He re-inspired me and I started my new R2O real estate business in February of 2010.

Dan Dubeau

Like David, I am originally from British Columbia, but well over 20 years ago I moved to the Halifax area of Nova Scotia. I spent two decades working as a financial planner helping clients manage their finances, reduce their income taxes, look after their RSPs and other investments. During that time, I noticed that people who could use the most help had the least access to those of us in the financial planning industry. Through David, I was introduced to some of his real estate ideas and was able to combine them with my own financial planning experience to come up with a win-win scenario that works very well in the Rent-to-Own category.

In 2006, I started to invest in the R2O sector. I got out of the financial planning field due to a certain frustration that had set in, borne out of the fact that we have no control over market forces. So if the Russian ruble is in crisis, if Bernie Madoff makes off with people's money, or if there's a mortgage meltdown in the US, nobody has control over these events.

We've seen a few times in the last ten years that people's money have been cut in half by drops in the stock market. Although the 1990s were very good for growth in investments, in the first decade of the 2000s, with all the ups and downs, there was very little money made despite the best efforts of financial advisors. When we look around, most people in the financial advice industry have very little knowledge or experience in real estate, and seldom put that out as an option for people to have good, steady, long-term growth that is not subject to fluctuations of outside influences as is the stock market.

After 23 years in the financial planning industry, switching to real estate investments was a big step. But it was a step that has given me control and peace of mind.

Dave Dubeau's website is www.ResultsHoldings.com

Dan Dubeau's website is www.AtlanticHomeSolutions.ca

CHAPTER 1

WHY REAL ESTATE INVESTING?

There are seven compelling reasons…

In this chapter, we'll talk about different investment options, the pros and cons of each, and why we think real estate rocks the house as the best investment for many Canadians.

Seeing that Dan has over 20 years of experience in the financial planning business, he is the bandleader for this chapter.

There are only two choices with investing: You can either "loan" or "own."

Loaning is what many people are familiar with, particularly with the banks.

When you put money in a savings account or a high-yield savings account, you're loaning your money to the bank. They give you a certain interest and then they put that money to work wherever and however they see fit.

Similarly, with other investments such as term deposits or GIC's, you're lending your money to the banks. They have it for an agreed upon duration, they're free to do whatever they want with it, and they will give you a specific rate of interest.

Keep in mind that when you're lending money in a GIC and similar investments, the bank figures out how much interest they're willing to pay relative to what they think they can make with the money, and the difference is their profit. It goes without saying that they want to pay you as little as possible to maximize their profit. And when investing in mutual funds, there are annual management fees – typically close to 2.5% – so that eats into your profit as well.

In fact, here's a real shocker: Studies indicate that management fees in Canada are the highest in the world. Think about it – mutual fund managers will make money off your investment regardless of whether you're making money or not. In today's financial environment, low return can be due to a significant portion of your wealth going into the managers' pockets with no guarantee of any kind as far as your own profit is concerned.

In essence, if you look at the individual holdings in your portfolio, they might have gone down about 17.5%; on top of that, a 2.5% management fee was added, so your total loss is close to 20%.

You can also have an investment with the government in the form of bonds and, in the private sector, corporate bonds. Here too, you're lending your money either to the government or a big corporation in return for a specific interest rate for a certain time period. Those investments are generally very safe. However, they tend to yield very low returns. There's a positive side to low interest rates, however – it's a good opportunity to borrow money for mortgages and other things. But, clearly, it's not so good if you're looking to invest into interest-bearing term deposits, GIC's or bonds.

Ownership Investments

The other category of investment is buying ownership of something, most commonly stocks or mutual funds. For example, you can buy a share of Royal Bank, Shell Oil, or some other company, and then your money will fluctuate with the ups and downs of the stock market and the fortunes of that particular company. Generally, over the long term they have a higher return than GIC's and other investments, but at any time your money could go down as well as up. If you could put a price on constant worry and uncertainty, then these kinds of investments are very expensive. We've seen this with a couple of severe drops in the stock markets. Huge quality companies have lost large amounts of value, 50% in many cases, and we can assure you that it does not feel good to see your life savings go drastically down – or disappear altogether. Sometimes they will recover, and other times they won't. This is to say that these types of investments have their good and bad points.

Lending investments are very safe, but they yield low returns. You're lucky if you're able to keep up with inflation. Ownership investments may have better returns. However, the price you pay is being willing to tolerate huge and unpredictable market fluctuations. You have to hope that you don't hit retirement just as your investment in a stock or mutual fund has gone down 30, 40, or 50%.

So "Loan" or "Own" are the two major choices of investment strategies.

BIG Benefit # 1: CONTROL

Real estate is an ownership type of investment, but unlike the stock market, you have much more control over it. You can control the neighbourhood where you invest in property. You can control what kind of people you allow to live in your property. You can somewhat control the income from the property. And when compared to many other real estate investing programs, with our R2O you have a profit already worked out and you know when and how much money you will receive. That's a big perk!

If you come away from this book with just one big idea (although we hope you'll learn more than that), it's to take control of your own finances and investments and not leave this vital responsibility in the hands of mutual fund salespeople (financial advisors) and the banks. They do not have your best interests at heart. Even if you choose not to move ahead with Rent-to-Own real estate investing, if you have control over your money, chances are you're going to get a much better return on your investment.

Also, with R2O, unlike the other types of investments we previously mentioned, you are cutting out the middleman. You're not paying anyone fees. You're collecting the full amount of the profit yourself.

BIG Benefit # 2: LEVERAGE

Another benefit of the R2O formula is leverage – the amount of money you can borrow as compared to the amount that you have to come up with personally. One of the beautiful attributes of real estate investing is that you have a relatively stable investment that you're able to leverage much, much more than you could by using stocks, mutual funds or even bonds. Typically, with blue chip stocks like bank shares or mutual funds, you might be able to borrow a dollar for every dollar that you have in. However, if you did borrow to that extent, you would be at risk of what's called "margin calls" – having to put up more money should the stock market decline.

The big concern here is that often those investments don't generate enough income to cover the borrowing cost and the dreaded margin call. This is what had people jumping out the windows in 1929 and during other market downturns.

In any case, chances are that the banks are not going to lend money to buy stocks or mutual funds to just anyone. The market is much too volatile and the risk of a loss is much too big.

However, banks LOVE real estate and, consequently, they love loaning money for it. If you have good credit, you can get into your own residence with 5% down, 10% max. There were times when you could get a house for nothing down.

For revenue-generating real estate, you now have to put down at least 20% of the purchase price of the property. What does this mean in terms of dollars? If you have access to $40,000 cash, you can buy a $200,000 investment property, and the banks would be happy to lend that to you because they consider real estate to be one of the best assets to secure an investment (and they're not subject to the margin calls of stocks).

When you get a mortgage from the banks, they are not looking at the value of your property every day and deciding whether or not you will need to come up with more money. They're happy if you put in 20% and they will be happy to lend you the other 80% – four dollars for every dollar that you put in. So, for every dollar you invested, you've got five dollars working for you. Compare that to stocks or mutual funds. The best you can hope to do with that $40,000, if you're willing to stomach the risk, is $80,000 working for you, but again, you would be subject to a dreaded margin call any time the stock market went down. You'd have to be prepared to come up with more money. The message here is clear: With real estate investing you have far more leverage and far more dollars working for you with far less risk.

BIG Benefit # 3: APPRECIATION

Let's go to the next big benefit of real estate vs. other investment options: Appreciation.

Most folks are familiar with this concept, but basically appreciation means how much the value of your property is going up year after year. This varies depending on the area of the country where you live. But this can be a huge profit potential when it comes to investing in real estate.

Here's an example: Let's say you purchased a $200,000 home. You had to put in $40,000 as a down payment, so you leveraged at

80%. And let's say that in the part of the country where you purchased the property, you can count on a 5% appreciation a year. Five percent appreciation on a $200,000 home means that it has gone up $10,000 in just one year.

That's not the only good news: Remember that you have only $40,000 of our own money invested in that $200,000 home. Of that $10,000 profit, none goes to the bank. Let's look at it from another angle: Even though the property itself went up "only" 5% in value in one year, that 5% appreciation means you have made a $10,000 profit on your $40,000 out-of-pocket investment – a 25% "cash-on-cash" return on your money in one year. That's nothing to sneeze at. Compared to GIC's, mutual funds and stocks, that's a HUGE value of leverage. Pretty sweet, isn't it?

That 5 %, by the way, is an average. In some areas of Canada, it's only 3%, in others it's as high as 8-10%. In Alberta during the mid 2000s, it was going up as high as 20-25% a year in certain regions. That's how real estate investors create massive wealth relatively quickly; quite often it's through appreciation. This is only one of the profit areas in real estate investing, but that's what people pay the most attention to because of the spectacular gains it generates.

BIG Benefit # 4: FORCED APPRECIATION

The other profit area in real estate that we'll talk about is something called "Forced Appreciation."

Forced Appreciation is when you purchase a property (perhaps one that is a little run down) and you make some fairly simple repairs, fix ups or cosmetic changes to it. After you have finished improving the property, you have also increased its value (quite often by two to three times more than what it cost you to do so).

In fact, we're looking at this type of property right now. It's from the 1970s, with a "lovely" salmon-coloured exterior (which – surprise, surprise – is not to everyone's taste).

Just because of the colour, the house is worth significantly less than the other properties on the block that are more updated.

Let's say you can buy this home for $200,000. However, by simply painting it a more neutral color, you can quite easily raise that value by as much as $10,000-$15,000. If you hire a painter, you spend a maximum of $3,000 or $4,000, but the property's value increases by $15,000. So all in all, it's still a very good deal for you. That is forced appreciation. Landscaping, taking out the shag carpets, putting in decent flooring, updating the kitchen – this kind of remodelling can "force" the value of the property higher.

We've seen people get fantastic results this way. They pick up a property that's out of date, a little shabby and run down, and it's amazing what sprucing up the place can do. You can get dramatic return on your money very quickly with forced appreciation. It will be even more profitable if you are handy and can do the repairs / upgrades yourself rather than hire contractors. But even if you have two left hands and end up paying someone else to do the work, you can still make good money off your property. And you are actually leveraging your time – you can use those extra hours to look for more deals instead of doing repairs yourself. That's smart.

BIG Benefit # 5: CASH FLOW

Now, let's talk a little bit about cash flow because that's another major benefit of real estate investing as compared to other investments. As a reminder, cash flow is the money that is left over at the end of the month after you've paid all of your expenses.

Average cash flow for properties varies from one area of the country to another. For instance, in Toronto, Edmonton, Calgary, and Vancouver, house prices have risen dramatically to the point that it is very difficult to rent them for a price that will generate any significant amount of positive cash flow. In fact, many landlords suffer from negative cash flow (their monthly expenses are greater than the income produced from rents). However, in other regions with less of a boom history, the rents generally allow you to have a little bit of a positive cash flow, even after you factor in all of your expenses, such as the mortgage, property taxes, insurance, and maintenance of the property. Again, this is one of the beauties of our R2O program. Because we're helping people become owners, one of the benefits is that we're able to get a higher than market rent, enabling us to have positive cash flow in any market, including those expensive cities that we mentioned.

Obviously, the lower you paid for the property and the higher the rent, the more cash flow you will have. For example, Winnipeg is a good area because the cost of properties is so much lower than in other regions and the rental payments are very good, resulting in positive cash flow that way. Generally, it's very difficult to have positive cash flow on single-family houses. You'll get better returns on multi-family, 3-plex, 4-plex, small apartment buildings or large apartment buildings.

But with our R2O formula, we are able to create phenomenal cash flow even from single-family houses. Actually, a very large portion of our total profits from R2O deals comes from monthly cash flow generated by these types of properties.

BIG Benefit # 6: MORTGAGE PAY-DOWN

Now, let's talk about mortgage pay-down. When we speak about the income from the renters, even if it's a break-even cash flow or a small positive cash flow, that income covers our typical expenses – the mortgage payment, property taxes, insurance, and any maintenance. Inside the mortgage payment is a combination of two items. One is the interest on the amount of money borrowed. The second component of several hundred dollars is the principle. Every month we'll actually be getting several hundred dollars richer because the mortgage is being paid down by a specified amount. Every month that goes by without any equity appreciation, you will own more and more of that property. You're becoming wealthier and wealthier just by paying your mortgage.

BIG Benefit # 7: TAX BENEFITS

The last moneymaking benefit of investment properties that we'll talk about in this chapter is depreciation or tax advantages from owning properties.

One thing that you can do with real estate as compared to other types of investments if you are in a positive cash flow situation, is to depreciate the building on your income taxes, take a write-off for the depreciation, and reduce your taxable income on that property from a taxable profit to zero.

This way, you don't have to pay any taxes until you sell the building at some point in the future. There are pros and cons to this strategy, but the nice point here is that it's preferable to defer taxes than to pay them and not have that money to work with. Most people would rather keep money in their wallets than put it in the government's pocket any earlier than they have to. So depreciation is a nice benefit of being an income property owner.

Another tax advantage worth mentioning is the benefit of capital gains, and how you're taxed on your real estate profits.

When you buy a property at one price and sell it in the future at a higher price, the difference that you make, your profit, is considered a capital gain. In Canada, capital gains have a tax advantage in that you only have to claim ½ of your capital gain on your tax return. So, if you make a $20,000 profit, only $10,000 of that is a taxable capital from the taxman's point of view. On the other hand, if you made $20,000 in interest income, you would have to pay tax on the full amount. A clear benefit of investing in real estate is that part of your profit is considered to be capital gains income, which has a significant tax advantage as compared to salary or interest income from other investment classes.

These are some of the different ways of making money with real estate. There are more, but in this book we're going to focus on the benefits of R2O real estate investing.

Again, the big idea is all about real estate investing in general. You've got much, much, much more control over your investment. You've got more ways of making profits from real estate than from other investment choices. In this chapter, we've talked about seven clear advantages and profit centers in R2O real estate investing. Compare that to a GIC, savings in the bank, stocks, or mutual funds. We're sure you'll agree that R2O is a better idea.

Hot Tip: Depreciating Tax Benefits

As we mentioned earlier, one of the advantages of real estate as compared to other types of investments, is that you can depreciate the property on your income taxes, thus reducing your taxable income to zero. If you do that, you won't have to worry about paying any taxes until you sell the property. Until that happens, you have all that extra cash lining your pockets rather than the government's. This way you have the money to invest in other deals, or do whatever else you want with it, at least temporarily. As you can see, depreciation is a nice benefit of being a rental property owner.

CHAPTER 2

WHAT IS R2O & WHY IT'S THE BEST WAY TO INVEST IN REAL ESTATE

Before we dig any deeper, let's go over the general concept of Rent-to-Owns as a real estate investment strategy. In Chapter 3, we're going to talk about three different kinds of R2O real estate investing, but right now let's focus on the concept in general: What it is and why there's such a big demand for it.

Rent-to-Own as we do it is when people like ourselves, who have the ability to purchase a home, partner with clients who don't qualify for a mortgage and possibly don't have the full amount for the down payment required to purchase a home, particularly if their credit is less than perfect. Even though these people may have a regular job and enough income to afford that property, the lending system is not ready to work with them yet. So, instead of buying the home, they rent it and have an option of purchasing it at a future date for a specified price, usually two, perhaps three years down the road.

Part of what they're paying every month for rent is being credited towards the purchase of the property when they buy it. This is a way for them to have a "forced" savings account to be used towards buying the home at the end of the deal. This "extra" money also allows you, the landlord, to charge “above average” rents (and generate cash flow) for a single family home.

Quite often the client has to also come up with some money up front, often called an option fee or a deposit. This money is usually credited towards his down payment when he eventually purchases the home – but it is forfeited if he does not complete the deal. It is an “insurance policy” of sorts for the investor, as it shows that the client is serious about buying the property, and not just renting it under false pretences.

The option deposit together with his monthly rental credits help the client pay most, if not all, of the costs associated with purchasing a home: Down payment, legal fees, property transfer taxes, etc. By giving him two to three years as a R2O term, you leave him enough time to pay the down payment in instalments and, hopefully, get his financial ducks in a row, so he will qualify for a mortgage. At that time, he can get traditional financing and buy the house at the end of his Rent-to-Own term.

That’s a quick overview of what the R2O concept entails.

Now let’s look at why there’s such a big demand for Rent-to-Own real estate investing.

In recent years, the U.S. banks had given mortgages to virtually anybody – qualified or not. They had what was called “ninja mortgages” – no income, no job applicants. They would be giving mortgages indiscriminately, which got packaged together, and, not surprisingly, the whole thing blew up. We didn’t have that problem in Canada, but we had a number of mortgage companies that worked with people with less than perfect credit. They were called B

Lenders. All of the mortgage rules tightened up when the problems from the States spilled over somewhat into Canada. Many of those B lender mortgage companies could no longer raise money to lend to people with less than stellar credit, so they went out of business.

All of a sudden, people who could have qualified for a B mortgage now find that there's nowhere for them to turn. They're being rejected left and right by banks, mortgage brokers and other lenders because the government has tightened up lending rules. You can no longer get a "nothing down" mortgage. You can no longer get "money-back" mortgages. You can no longer get a mortgage with a 40-year amortization. Consequently, there are a lot of people (some numbers indicate that as many as 40% of Canadians can't afford a mortgage payment) who are interested in being home-owners, but can't qualify for a mortgage. They've saved some money towards a home. They have good jobs and income. Although they would have qualified for a mortgage a couple of years ago, in today's economic reality, they don't.

In a nutshell then, R2O entails renting a house to a client with the option for him to purchase that property in the future. Part of his monthly rental payment is credited towards the purchase of that property (and don't forget that he had given you a significant option deposit as well). The idea is to give him time to get his finances straightened out to qualify for a traditional mortgage, so that he is able to buy the property in the future. That's the "big" picture of how it all works.

Now let's move to the pros and cons of Rent-to-Own real estate investing. We'll talk about all the advantages first and then we'll cover the flip side of the coin.

Pros of R2O Real Estate Investing

Let's start by talking about the cash flow situation first. As you recall, in Chapter One we talked about cash flow as being one of the profit centers of real estate investing. We mentioned that getting positive cash flow from a single-family home is extremely difficult. However, with Rent-to-Own real estate investing, it's very easy to get several hundred dollars, even up to $1,000 a month in positive cash flow from just one house!

Let's talk about that for a little bit.

It may be hard to believe that people would be happy to pay a higher than normal rent, or a "premium" rent as we call it. But the point to remember is that the portion exceeding the normal rent is really a "forced" savings component that benefits them. As we mentioned earlier, that is the part that we're going to credit back to them at the end of the program. A normal rent may or may not generate cash flow, but if we add a premium to it, the savings component, it gives us a positive cash flow regardless of the market that we're in. You simply cannot get that kind of cash flow with normal (non-R2O) rental properties.

Minimal Property Management Hassles

Another huge advantage of the R2O plan is that you're dealing with a very different kind of tenant. Traditionally, when you're doing a normal rental, your tenants are looking at your property as temporary digs, until they can get into something better. Those people are the toilet and tenant nightmare stories that you hear so much about from disgruntled landlords.

With R2O real estate investing, especially the way we do it, it's a completely different story. (We are going to talk about this in more detail in Chapter Three). Our client is not a typical renter – he is going to be much less of a pain in the neck to deal with. He is looking at the property as his own because he is paying money in to buy it in the future. He is going to treat the house with much more care than an average in-and-out renter. He is not going to call you in the middle of the night; he'll be doing repairs and improvements on the property instead of destroying it as other tenants often do.

That's what attracted us to the Rent-to-Own model in the first place: People making plans for the house to be their own. They're painting it the colors they like. They're making improvements. They're getting their children established in the local schools. They know that this is going to be their own home, and they are very committed to making it the best property that they can. So instead of calls for you to come fix this or that, you're getting calls like "Can I lay down tile in the kitchen?" or things of that nature. So it's a much more positive experience for both the tenant and the landlord. Clearly, getting rid of maintenance hassles is one of the main advantages of R2Os.

Going along with this line of thought, let's talk about the issue of property maintenance. We already established that we're dealing with a different kind of tenants because they're future homebuyers committed to making the property their own. Part of the deal is that instead of having a traditional tenant agreement or a tenant contract, we've got a lease contract on this property. This is very important to understand. Because this is a lease and not a tenancy, our client is responsible for all the maintenance.

That's a huge difference. If the tenant looks after the property, makes improvements to it, and does some of the forced appreciation that we referred to earlier, he will get the full benefit of that once the house is his.

If we set a price and the tenant improves the property or property prices appreciate higher than the agreed upon final sale price, the tenant gets all the benefit of that as well. He gets all the perks, but also the inconveniences. He has to take care of the 3:00 a.m. clogged toilet and other problems that may arise. Not you! He understands that up front and knows it's his responsibility. He knows he has to solve all the property-related problems himself and NOT call you.

Needless to say, that's a huge benefit to you, the landlord. You don't have to be worried about going away for the weekend and the tenant calling you because the screen door is falling off. That's his headache, not yours. In a typical (non-R2O) scenario, maintenance problems in single-family homes can wipe out all the appeal of real estate investing.

So here's the kicker: The fact that you've got a lease agreement instead of a normal tenancy virtually eliminates all of the typical landlord headaches. We've met many frustrated, fed up landlords over the years who are sick and tired of dealing with tenants. You, on the other hand, are in for a largely hassle-free landlord experience!

Pre-Determined Profits

We previously mentioned the cash flow, so let's talk again about profit potential of Rent-to-Own deals. Another huge pro of R2O investing as opposed to conventional real estate investing is the profit potential - the defined profit that you know you're going to get when you complete the program.

Most rental property owners don't have an exit plan. They buy a property, they rent it out, they may or may not have a positive cash flow – often they don't. In some cases, they even have to subsidize a property if an unexpected maintenance issue comes up. Their hope is on the appreciation when they sell at some point in the future. That may or may not work out as well as they had hoped in the beginning because nobody is guaranteeing any kind of an exit price.

What about R2O? We don't enter into a deal unless we know exactly how much money we're going to make out of it. We know in advance what we need, what we're going to get from our monthly cash flow, and what we're going to make over the two or three year program. We don't do the deal unless the profit numbers fit within the guidelines of what we're looking for.

As you can see, we have a huge advantage over traditional landlords because we don't have to worry about unexpected maintenance expenses that in many cases can wipe out much of the profit that you expect to make in a conventional landlord situation. We don't have to worry very much about the market either. We've set an exit price and we have the cash flow. We know going in what we're going to make on that particular property, and over what time period we're going to make it.

Any way you slice it, it's a wonderful scenario. We're getting money up front from our client. We're getting a positive cash flow every month. We're making cash at the end of the deal as well when the client buys us out. We're making money all the way through. Compare that to other forms of real estate investing where quite often (especially with single-family homes) you're actually going to have to subsidize that sucker and you're just praying for appreciation to solve your problems and give you a profit. That's a gamble, a speculation. Then, you've also got normal tenants in there who are causing damage and maintenance issues. What happens if three or four years down the road you need to sell the house and the market has taken a dip?

Quite often, when people are investing in real estate, it's an emotional thing. They see a lot of people investing in real estate and (supposedly) making BIG money from it. They get all excited and they jump into the market, usually at the absolute worst time, when housing prices are at their peak. When the market takes a dip, they're out of luck and are often in a negative cash flow situation. Then they get a few nightmare tenants and end up miserable, frustrated and desperate with their investment, and to add insult to injury, they're subsidizing the whole thing with their own money!

With our R2O program, everything is clearly defined from the start – both the entry and exit points. It's very clear. We know what we're paying today and what our cash flow is going to be in the future. We know what we need to get up front from our client, how long the process is going to take, and what our end price is going to be ahead of time. We've got spreadsheets that show us exactly how the whole deal is going to work. So that's the big advantage of R2O versus traditional real estate investing in rental properties.

In addition, we don't have the risk of wondering whether someone will be willing to come along and buy this place in two or three years, or whatever our time frame is. We have a buyer-in-training in the home already. Those are the two major risks that everybody is looking at when buying a single-family home as a rental property. We've taken care of those risks. On top of that, we get a premium cash flow. What's not to like?

Those are the main pros of Rent-to-Own real estate investing: Defined entry and exit strategy. Cash flow. But what happens if the deal doesn't work out?

Let's assume our future buyer, our client, isn't able to purchase the property or decides to leave ahead of time. Basically, we're not in a bad situation at all because if he does that, he forfeits the initial up-front deposit, as well as any of the rental credits he has accumulated. We are able to keep all of that cash flow. The client knows all that before getting into the program. We can turn around and do the same deal over again with someone else. In essence, our cost of the property has been reduced by the amount of the up-front deposit and the monthly credits that we keep. Our cost is down, while the property has probably appreciated in value, so we are actually benefiting from that unlikely scenario.

Now let's talk a little bit about the negatives. Before we do, we want to stress that, in our experience, there are far fewer "cons" than "pros." That's why we're in this business.

The Cons of the R2O Process

The biggest negative of Rent-to-Own as compared to other types of real estate investing is having to replace our portfolio every two to three years. It's not completely passive. A lot of folks, when they get into traditional buying-and-holding real estate investing, are just amassing as many properties as they can, have a bit of a cash flow or try to break even.

They're looking at the longer-term scenario. R2O, on the other hand, is usually two to three years. You're in and you're out. We see that as a pro, but it can also be a negative because you have to find new deals and clients on a regular basis to keep this business going if you want to maintain cash flow.

The other negative would be finding an ideal client every two to three years. Let's talk about that for a minute.

When a typical tenant begins a rental agreement, he just needs to have, at best, a damage deposit and the first month's rent. You're not at all concerned about his ability to qualify for a mortgage. With R2O, we put a lot more work into pre-qualifying our future buyers (clients) because we want somebody who is extremely likely to succeed and who will be able to buy this property in the time frame that we have agreed upon. That's why we must have a much more detailed screening process. We look at their finances and their credit.

Those are the two big cons in the business.

For us, the goal is cash flow. We'll be using some of the cash flow that's spun off from this business to buy longer-term buy-and-hold properties. In our case, we'll focus on a commercial and multi-family housing.

CHAPTER 3

THREE DIFFERENT R20 STRATEGIES

Welcome to Chapter 3. Here, we're going to talk about the three different and distinct R2O strategies.

The first one is what we call the "traditional" Rent-to-Own.

R2O Strategy # 1: Traditional Rent-to-Own

This is how it works: You have a frustrated landlord who's sick and tired of owning a particular property or properties for any number of reasons, some of which we talked about in the previous chapter.

It could be that the property itself has some challenges. It might be outdated or otherwise a pain in the ass to rent. Or maybe it's very difficult to sell this piece of property traditionally. It could also be the fact that the landlord is having problems with tenants from hell. "Come fix my toilet," "My screen door is broken," and so on. He'd rather not have those tenant problems anymore and who can blame him? So he's looking for a way to sell the property and get the full value or a premium price for it, but he's not able to achieve that by selling the house traditionally.

However, if he can make a deal with Rent-to-Own clients, he can generally save himself the real estate commissions, which can be a significant amount – typically 5 or 6%, not including the taxes that might be tacked onto the real estate fees. For these reasons, R2O is a very attractive option to get out of a property that the landlord no longer wants to own. He finds a potential buyer, makes an arrangement with him, and sets a future price that the client will have to pay two or three years down the road.

There are several ways for the owner to decide how much of the rent would be applied towards the final price as a rental credit.

That part, by the way, gets negotiated with the client directly. Typically, landlords will charge a deposit that is much higher than the normal rental damage deposit. Depending on the area of the country, the standard rental deposit is anywhere from half the month's rent to a full month's rent.

On the other hand, when doing a Rent-to-Own agreement, you're trying to get as much money as you possibly can from the tenant to make sure he is serious about purchasing the property in the future. That's because this deposit is non-refundable so he will forfeit it if he reneges on the deal. Now, if this type of property is unique or, for whatever reason, not everyone's cup of tea, like the one we mentioned at the beginning of this chapter, this initial deposit will not be as high as it normally would be in other R2O arrangements. But you're still looking at $3,000 to $5,000 down. That's nothing to sneeze at.

Keep in mind that there could be some problems associated with these traditional Rent-to-Owns. As an example, quite often neither the landlord nor the tenant has done this type of arrangement before, so they're flying by the seat of their pants. They could enter into verbal rather than written agreements, which sounds fine in the beginning, but then something goes wrong somewhere along the line, and someone loses out.

We've seen a number of these deals become problematic because they were not done in a business-like manner. The client understood the arrangement one way and the landlord had something completely different in mind. This was a recipe for disaster. That is one potential problem with these traditional R2Os, especially if they're not operated in a professional, business-like manner by a savvy real estate investor, but rather, by an amateur with a steep learning curve. (That's one more compelling reason to keep reading this book!)

Above-mentioned problems aside, Rent-to-Own can be a very effective way of selling a problematic house for a good price.

Probably the biggest challenge we see with this type of property is finding a client who will be satisfied to live in a "quirky" home. It does take somewhat of a visionary (and a handy one at that) to take on an outdated or an otherwise wonky property and make it his own. So that would be the number one challenge with this type of property.

We actually speak from experience here because we worked with somebody who had a property on the market for a number of months. It was a slow period of time in real estate, so the house was sitting vacant for a while waiting for someone to fall in love with it.

It was a nice enough property, but there were other competing houses available in the area. The owners weren't getting the price they wanted for it, so we took it over. It took us longer than we expected to find a client because when you're trying to fit a square peg into a round hole, it's not easy. In fact, it takes time, patience, and many efforts to find somebody who will want that particular property rather than the alternative, which we'll be discussing towards the end of this chapter.

It's easy to get disheartened when you have an empty property sitting there for a period of time, not generating any income. You'll have to go through a lot of tire kickers on this deal before you find the right person for it. But keep in mind that once a buyer does show up, you're going to get a much higher than normal deposit on the property and you're going to get a higher than normal rent on it as well.

Another thing about the traditional Rent-to-Own is that these deals tend to give the whole R2O business a bad name. That's because in some cases you've got very unscrupulous landlords who basically do this as a "churn and burn" way of making money.

Here is how they do it: These sleazy landlords have a property and they put it out as a R2O. They get someone in there for a couple of thousand dollar option deposit, and they don't give a crap whether this person will ever qualify for a mortgage or not.

Usually these are very short one-year or 18-month deals and the tenants have put up a chunk of change up front. Part of that is going to be credited towards the purchase of the house IF they can buy it in the 12 or 18-month time frame. In the meantime, they're getting absolutely no support. Again, the landlord doesn't care whether the clients qualify for the mortgage at the end or not. In fact, he prefers that they don't because that way he can kick them out and find another sucker for the property (and another deposit) every 12 or 18 months.

This allows the sleaze bag to have his mortgage paid down by an unwitting tenant, and all the property appreciation goes to him as well.

In addition to that, he has been getting a much higher than normal market rent and great cash flow on the dump.

As you can see, sometimes bad guys do win. Unfortunately, this scenario gives R2Os a bad name.

This sneaky but deliberate strategy is part of the reason why more than half of traditional Rent-to-Own deals fall through. Well, what do you expect? They're set up to fail from the start.

Needless to say, that's not the kind of R2Os we're involved in and would ever touch. We want to create a win-win situation based on transparency and honesty.

We're only bringing up this "sleazy landlord" scenario so you know what's out there lurking in the shadows. When you hear negative things about Rent-to-Own, most of the time it has to do with this strategy. Unfortunately, as in any business, a few bad apples can taint the entire barrel. Thankfully, the vast majority of the people in this business are not scumbags.

Now that we got that off our chests, let's move on to sandwich leases. No, it has nothing to do with food per se, although, as you will see, it can be very appetizing.

R2O Strategy # 2: Sandwich Leases

Actually, it's a fantastic strategy but not always easy. A sandwich lease is where you find property sellers who are motivated enough to lease the property to you with the option for you to purchase it. You lease the property from them. You're responsible for the payments. You're responsible for the maintenance on the property. But then you turn around and sublet that same house to your client with an option for him to purchase it from you at a higher price. So you're kind of the middleman in there. That's why it's called a sandwich. You're in the middle between the original home seller and your client, who is going to be the final buyer. You're making the whole deal happen and you're making some good money with that. We speak from experience here because we've tried this strategy ourselves.

In theory, it sounds like a very good plan. It can work really well. In fact, this was actually one of our better deals. This is how it worked: We found a very frustrated landlord who was just sick and tired of having problematic tenants time after time. The poor bastard had been hit four or five times in a row by nightmare tenants. He finally put the place up for sale but the market was soft so the house didn't sell.

We decided to be knights in shining armour. We came to him with this sandwich solution and he agreed to it. We said we would cover his costs – mortgage payment, taxes, insurance, and maintenance. We would turn around and find clients for the property and sublet it to them. We would be charging them more than what we would be paying the landlord ourselves. That's how we would be making money. There was an option to purchase the property for a set price and then give our clients the possibility to buy it from us at a higher price – again, to make money. Everything was done with the maximum of transparency. We all knew what we were getting into and what profit we would be taking out of it. The landlord was keen just to have the headache taken off his plate. He didn't want to deal with this property anymore.

We advertised, filtered and sorted through many different people, finally finding a worthy client for this property. There was a fair difference between the rent we were getting and the rent we were paying the landlord – $400 or $500 a month lining our pockets. In an agreed-upon time frame, the client purchased the property from us and we kept the difference between what he paid us and what we paid the original owner. It was a win-win situation and we all lived happily ever after.

That's the nice thing about these sandwich leases. As we mentioned earlier, one of the pitfalls of the traditional Rent-to-Own is that the people involved don't have any experience with it. They don't know how to put a deal together. So if you come in with your expertise, as we did in the example we just cited, you're going to be rewarded in terms of revenue.

Obviously, you have to be knowledgeable and go into the deal armed to the teeth. Get all the legal forms, all the nitty-gritty. Basically, you're saying to the landlord, "I'm willing to look after your property for you. I'm willing to take the problem away from you, and solve it for you. You're going to get a nice price. All you have to do is sit back and wait a couple of years for your money."

A nice thing about this for you is that you can control a property with no money out of your own pocket. That's the beauty of the sandwich lease from the perspective of the R2O expert (which you will hopefully become yourself). Here's the bottom line: You can make a nice profit without a cent out of your pocket. You're being paid just because you have the expertise that the current homeowner doesn't. You're connecting him with the client and looking after the property in the meantime. So again, it's a very good example of a win-win situation.

In the case we mentioned above, the homeowner was a typical landlord with normal tenancy agreements with his tenants. We switched that around and said, "Okay, look at this. This is an ideal situation for you. You don't have to worry about maintenance or getting complaints in the middle of the night. You don't have to worry about anything happening to the property. If anything goes wrong at the end of the day, I'm the guy that's on the hook."

You can almost see the frazzled and frustrated landlord morph into a happy camper. And, of course, it's not a shabby deal for us either. We got into this property with just one dollar to make it legal. That was it. One dollar. Then we had it spaced out so that our actual lease agreement didn't start for two or three months. That gave us a little bit of a leeway to try and find the ideal client, and that's what we did.

By now the advantages of the sandwich R2O should be clear as a bell. As a professional real estate investor, you can get into these kinds of deals with no money down. You might have to spend a little bit on home inspections and on making sure your legal documentations are all up to speed. But you don't have to put 20% down to get into this deal. The other big advantage is that there's a fair market for this option, especially if you're in an area where the housing market is a little bit slumped and slow. It will be a snap to find people who are interested in this arrangement.

In fact, just very recently, we did a little promotion ourselves in the Kamloops area - a small market of about 85,000 people. In about three weeks, close to 75 homeowners responded to our marketing; they were all interested in talking about this concept. How many of them will actually get involved in sandwich leases, we can't say with any certainty. But we think that at least four or five will run with it and make fistfuls of money.

Exciting? Yes. But don't lose sight of the potential pitfalls. They're pretty much the same as with a traditional "Rent to Own" program: You've got the property and you're trying to find the person who likes the house enough to come up with some cash and do a R2O deal with it. This is not always as easy as it sounds. There's no magic bullet.

Still, when it does work (as it does in many, many cases), the big benefit is that you're in control of the property with no money out of your pocket. (We mentioned this before but are repeating because it's important to get this point across). Once you become skilled at sandwich leases, you can do an infinite number of these deals. And if you use marketing, you'll have homeowners and property sellers seeking you out on a regular basis. You can put property deals together with no limit because you don't have to bring in your own money, as compared to putting 20% down on a conventional deal.

R2O Strategy # 3: Client's Choice

Now, let's have a look at scenario number three, which is our favourite. It is the "client's choice" method of R2O.

It's a similar concept to a conventional Rent-to-Own but with one very big difference. The client's choice, as the name suggests, means that you qualify the client as someone who will be able to complete the deal satisfactorily within the two or three-year time period. Based on that, you determine what price range is suitable for his budget; in other words, what kind of home he can afford.

Then you allow the client to choose from all the properties on the market – private sales, MLS through realtors, whatever. In essence, he himself is choosing the house he's going to live in.

Once the home has been chosen and checked out, you buy it on his behalf, getting all the option fees up front. You will charge him the appropriate rent. Obviously, you sort all of these things out prior to letting the client select a property, so he knows what price range he should be looking at, what it's going to cost him on a monthly basis, and what it's going to cost at the end. Everything is transparent, remember? With this approach, you have the greatest likelihood of success, the best chance of finding a qualified future buyer, and a happy ending for everyone.

Here it is again, in a nutshell: With the client's choice method, instead of starting with a house first and trying to find a client to fit into it, we're starting with the client first and we're letting him find the house he likes and can afford. We're buying it for him (either ourselves or with our investors – we talk about this in further chapters) and Rent-to-Own it to him. This way, the client is more involved in the whole process, much more motivated and committed.

The flipside? You have to come up with a 20% down payment or you have to be working with investors to pull this off. With a sandwich lease, you don't have to use your own funds. However, you've got a lot more challenges finding the ideal client for that property, whereas this particular option practically sells itself.

To sum up: The two preferred R2O methods are the sandwich lease and the client's choice.

The benefit of the sandwich lease is that you don't have to put any money in. The difficulty is that it's more challenging to find a qualified client for the property. With the client's choice system, on the other hand, it's much easier to find qualified clients, but you're either putting up your own money or have to partner with investors.

Hot Tip: Learn What Not To Do

Whether you're interested in a traditional R2O, a sandwich, or a client's choice, you can gain a valuable perspective on the business by knowing what kind of practices to avoid. Take a look at your local Kijiji or Craigslist's R2O categories and reply to some of the ads offering Rent-to-Owns. Are their practices something you want to emulate or avoid because these programs are clearly operated by unscrupulous landlords? Even a negative example can be a good learning experience.

CHAPTER 4

R2O PROFIT POTENTIAL – SHOW ME THE MONEY!

Show me the money? Now we're talking! Let's jump into how much money you can make as a professional R2O real estate investor.

To explain the concept better, we're going to use a hypothetical property. We have chosen a $250,000 house, which is fairly realistic as a starter home for the Kamloops area.

If you're in a high-priced city like Vancouver, $250,000 will probably buy you just a couple of bricks. But if you live in the middle of Timbuktu, Saskatchewan, that money could get you a mansion!

In this example, we're going to be the investors. We'll be putting up the money for that hypothetical $250,000 home and working on a 5% per year appreciation on the property value. If this is going to be an investment property, CMHC rules say that we have to put 20% down, which means we can get 80% financing. We have to come up with $50,000 (20% of $250,000) plus some extra money to cover closing costs.

In many provinces, especially in Nova Scotia and British Columbia, there's also a property transfer tax to factor into your total purchase cost. So to be conservative, let's add another 2% of the purchase price for closing costs.

Adding up all of the above, the total cash we have to come up with to purchase this property is $55,000 (20% down + 2% closing costs and taxes)

Remember, the purchase price is $250,000 and appreciation is 5% per year. So that means that at the end of a two-year Rent-to-Own term, we're going to sell the house to our client for $275,000.

As far as a non-refundable option deposit from the client, it would be 4% of the purchase price, which would be $10,000 in this example. And we're going to rent this house to the client for $2,000 per month, which is a premium rent because this home would normally go for $1,600.

However, as we explained to you in previous chapters, a portion of that premium rent is going to be treated as a rental credit and is credited back to the client at the end of the program. In this case, we would be crediting him $400 a month towards his down payment once the client buys the property. So his net rent over that period, once rental credits are factored in, would be $1,600 a month – very close to what he would pay for the normal rent. But for our cash flow purposes, we are collecting $2,000 a month.

Are you with us so far?

Okay, let's crunch some numbers. Over the two-year time frame for the whole deal, $400 a month x 24 months is $9,600 in rental credits. The client has paid his non-refundable option deposit of $10,000 up front, so all together he will have paid $19,600 towards the purchase of the property. Again, that money will be credited towards his down payment and closing costs when he buys the house from us in two years (and he will need those credits to satisfy the mortgage people).

What is our profit at the end of this deal? Let's walk through it: We put in $55,000 up front as our cash investment. We have immediately received $10,000 non-refundable option deposit from our client, so out of $55,000, that's almost a 20% return right there. Sweet.

Let's say we're going to get a 4% mortgage from the bank. At the time of this writing, that's actually a little bit high as you can get mortgages right now for 3%. But let's be conservative and go with 4%, just for the sake of this example. We're also saying that we're appreciating the house at 5% a year. Now we typically appreciate our properties at 6% a year, but, again, we want to be conservative so these numbers are more relevant to whichever province you live in. With this calculation, our net monthly cash flow is $780. In other words, when we deduct the cost of our mortgage, property taxes and insurance, we're left over with $780 a month.

This is how we got this figure: Our client is paying us $2,000 a month. Out of that, the monthly payment on a $200,000 mortgage, amortized over 35 years at 4% is $882 a month. In addition, we estimate about $250 a month in property taxes on a home of this value, plus about $88 a month for landlord insurance, fire insurance, and things like that. So $2,000 minus those three things – the mortgage, the property taxes, and the insurance – leaves us with a positive cash flow of $780 a month.

Example:
Sample $250,000 home.

Income:
$2,000 per month in rent.

Expenses:
$882.00 per month for the mortgage payment.
$250.00 per month for property taxes.
$88.00 per month for insurance.

Total monthly income: $2,000.00
Total monthly expenses: ($1,220.00)

Total Net monthly cash flow: $780.00

And it is important to remember that the client has agreed to look after all the maintenance, so that's one thing we don't have to budget for. We also don't have to worry about the utilities because the client is paying for those as well. We, on the other hand, are paying the property taxes, which are quite often included in the mortgage payment.

Now, just to give you some perspective if you're new to this game, we can tell you that quite a few investors would be thrilled to get $50 to $75 a month positive cash flow per door. If that's the case, income from this one house is the equivalent of 10 traditional "buy-and- hold" rental properties!

This is only one of the profit centers of real estate investing. But we figured out a way with Rent-to-Own to increase our monthly cash flow more than 10 times – 10 TIMES! That's more than what your typical buy-and-hold investors are getting with their rental properties. Unless you're Bill Gates or Warren Buffet, $780 a month in your pocket is nothing to sneeze at.

Okay, let's go back to our cash cow of a house and look at what our TOTAL PROFIT will be for this deal. Everything is going according to plan. At the end of the two years, our client is all set up with financing. He has paid in almost $20,000 through his initial deposit, non-refundable option deposit, and the rental credits. He purchased the house from us. So again, to remind you where our profits come from, the lion's share come in up front and during the two-year R2O process: We've received our $10,000 from the option deposit. We've received $780 a month for 24 months. That's $18,720 in positive cash flow over that time. When everything is said and done, between the $275,000 final sale price and all of the rental credits, the option fee credit, and the mortgage pay-down, we're going to come out with an extra $5,000 at the very end of the deal as well. Our total profit is just over $34,500 for this two-year deal; a $34,500 return on our $55,000 initial deposit adds up to 63%.

What other safe investments can give you that kind of return?

Deal Summary: Total Profit.

Initial Purchase Price:	$250,000.00
Initial Cash Investment:	$55,000.00
(down payment plus closing costs & taxes)	
Initial Option Deposit from client:	$10,000.00
Net monthly Cash Flow from the deal:	$18,720.00
($780/month x 24 months)	

Final cash-out at end of the deal:

Final Sale Price to Client:	$275,000.00
Less Initial Cash Investment:	- $55,000.00
Less final mortgage amount owed:	- $194,500.00
Less Initial Deposit Credit:	- $10,000.00
Less Rental Credits:	- $9,600.00
Remaining profit from sale:	$5,900.00

Total Profit:

Initial Option Deposit:	$10,000.00
Monthly Cash Flow:	$18,720.00
Remaining profit from sale:	$5,900.00
Total profit from deal:	$34,620.00

Keep in mind, too, that we're being intentionally conservative. We're using a higher interest rate than what we're actually paying for mortgages right now. If we made our calculations based on a more realistic 3% mortgage rate, it would increase our profit by another $5,000 or so.

And it gets even better. If we get a 6% appreciation instead of five, that would raise our profits by another $5,000 or $6,000 as well. Again, the amount you can calculate for appreciation depends on which area of the country you're in, and what's happening in your local real estate market.

Right now, let's talk some more about these R2O numbers as compared to profits yielded by a typical real estate transaction in the same short period of time.

With this method, you have an investor buying a $250,000 single family home on a speculation that he would get some appreciation on the property, have decent tenants, and low maintenance. Maybe or maybe not, because there is some risk attached to each of these factors. As we mentioned in previous chapters, "decent" tenants are certainly not a given, and you can't count on low maintenance costs either, especially with older houses. You know Murphy's Law: "Anything that can go wrong, will go wrong." Okay, so that might be a slight exaggeration, but very few landlords can honestly say they've had a hassle-free tenancy.

In our case, we've eliminated much of the risk and many of the problems that typical landlords endure. We've set up a system where we get premium rent, and consequently, premium cash flow. Helping our cash flow is the fact that our client is taking care of all the maintenance so we don't have that cost. In addition, we have agreed on a price in advance, so we know what we're going to make from this sweet deal if everything goes as planned. In the vast majority of cases, by the way, everything does go as planned. It's a rare situation under our client's choice plan that the buyers walk away from their dream home and lose credits and option fees that they have invested in the property. Murphy's Law can strike in this scenario too, but really, it's very rare. We have a much higher likelihood of success than of failure. We can relax, sleep easily, and basically laugh all the way to the bank. Never underestimate the power of peace of mind. And that's a huge advantage over the conventional buy-and-hold rental investing.

Now let's look at the scenario where we have an investor putting up the money for the R2O deal instead of us. If we work with an investor-partner, then what kind of profits are we looking at?

Why are we bringing up the idea of working with money partners / investors? Because after reading this chapter about how much money can be made in R2O, you might get so enthused that you'd like to do several of these deals at once, or one after another!

But unless you've got very deep pockets, you're going to run out of down payment money sooner or later. Now, having said that, we would suggest that you use your own money for your first one or two deals. This is where some R2O investors disagree with us. However, we do think you should use your own funds for the first couple of deals so you can go through the whole process, learn the ropes, and show your future money partners that you too have your skin in the game, that you're very serious about this, and that you're willing to put your money where your mouth is.

Let's use the same numbers as above – a $250,000 home – but instead of putting up the money ourselves, we're going to get an investor or a money partner to come up with $55,000 ($50,000 down payment plus 2% for closing costs). All the other numbers we used in the previous example stay the same, except that we are going to have to pay our money partner / investor a return on his investment. How much? In this case, we would pay him 12.65% per year, compounded for the two-year term.

Let's crunch the numbers again so you understand how we arrived at this percentage. Since we're not bringing in any of our own money, the investor puts in the entire $55,000 down payment. Our contribution to the deal is non-monetary but nevertheless important: We are managing the investment, looking after the house, and taking on all the risks associated with that particular property. All the investor has to do with our program is sit back for two years and wait for the return on his money. At 12.65% compounded, his $55,000 will have grown in value to $69,795 at the end of the two years.

When our client buys the house from us for $275,000, then after you subtract the legal fees, credit his option deposit and rental credits, pay off the mortgage, and give the investor $69,795, (which again, is a 12.65% return per year compounded on his $55,000 initial investment), then we're left with just a few hundred dollars at the end.

Final Sale Price to Client:	$275,000.00
Less Payback to money-partner:	- $69,795.00
Less final mortgage amount owed:	- $194,500.00
Less Initial Deposit Credit:	- $10,000.00
Remaining profit from sale:	$705.00

But wait. Before you run for the woods, remember that during that two-year period we have collected $18,720 as net rent, which amounts to $780 a month positive cash flow that we've received after paying off mortgage and other costs. So again, for no money out of our own pocket, for our expertise, for finding and managing the property, for finding the client, we're walking away with nearly $19,000, out of which we received $10,000 up front and the remainder on a monthly basis out of this positive cash flow.

Your Total Profit on the Deal, when working with an investor:

Initial Option Deposit:	$10,000.00
Net monthly Cash Flow*:	$9,120.00
Remaining profit from sale:	$ 705.00
Your Total Profit from the deal:	$19,825.00

*This is after you deduct the $9,600 in rental credits from the $18,720 in total cash flow from the rent over the 24-month period.

That's a hefty profit if you consider that you put none of your own money into this deal, just your time and expertise.

We used a $250,000 house as an example here, but if you're in a bigger city and looking at $300,000 or $400,000 properties, then your profit is going to be correspondingly higher. By the same token, if you're in an area where houses are less costly, what profit can you expect? And, how do you get more profit out of your deals in regions like Nova Scotia, where starter homes range between $170,000 and $215,000?

In this case, you would put in less money up front, so you'll pay out 12.65% on $45,000 instead of $55,000. Your output of money is lower, as is your net profit, but the percentage of your return remains the same.

Speaking for ourselves, we're looking for at least a $20,000 profit per deal on our R2O properties. That number is based on today's interest rates, which are a little lower than what we're using in these examples. We also use 6% appreciation, instead of 5%. But even if we're conservative with our math, the numbers we get are still very profitable. If we continue to be able to get mortgages with these low interest rates, which are very favourable for real estate investors, then the profits will be even higher.

"But wait!"(Just like they say in the old "Ginsu-knife" ads)... "There's More!" We have arrangements with some real estate agents where we receive 50% of their net commissions, which can add another $2,000 or $3,000 per transaction to the net profit as well!

Why would they give us half of their commission? In a nutshell, this is the easiest job a real estate agent will ever have because we're telling him "Take these people, they're pre-qualified, we're going to buy the house for them, and just help them find a property they like that fits within this price range. If it checks out okay with our home inspector, we'll buy it!" It's a very easy job for them. It's a slam-dunk deal, and they have zero marketing costs involved because we have delivered them a client on a silver platter!

Now you will have to talk with your real estate agent about how to do it, because the rules vary from one province to another. But even if the agent tells you he can't do this type of a commission split, don't believe it. Whether it's called a marketing fee or something else, it's definitely possible.

Once you seriously get into this R2O business, are buying multiple properties and giving these guys repeat business, they'll be happy to work with you.

Let's face it! Real estate is a tough business, especially these days when properties are not exactly selling like hotcakes. Plus, they no longer have a monopoly on the MLS. There are a lot of discount realtors coming into the game, as well as sale-by-owner-type services. In Kamloops where we have a population of 85,000, there are over 310 realtors! That's crazy! And if you look at the statistics from the real estate board, approximately 80% of the people who get a real estate license in any given year will be out of the business within three years.

All this is to say that if they see you as a reliable partner who is helping them make a buck, they'll be happy to cooperate with you. If they're smart, they'll recognize an opportunity when they see one and jump on it before their competitors do.

So there you have it – now we have "Shown You the Money."

Let's move on to Chapter 5, where we're going to talk about our ideal client.

Hot Tip / Resource:

We showed you the numbers so you know what profit potential there is in the R2O program. But we want to make it even easier for you to figure out what your costs are.

Go to www.RentToOwnProfits.com to get a FREE copy of our R2O deal analyzer along with over $268.85 in other valuable R2O resources! It's all there, so you don't have to crunch and re-crunch the numbers manually each time. Copy our spreadsheet and you can use it over and over again!

Chapter 5

Who's Your Ideal Client?

Before we start answering this question, let's go back to a statistic we cited earlier on: As many as 40% of all Canadians who can afford a mortgage don't qualify for one right now. What this means is simple: a huge portion of the housing market consists of renters – nearly half of all Canadians are tenants rather than homeowners.

Our ideal client is someone who is among those 40% who would like to be homeowners and who can afford the mortgage payment, but for whatever reason, don't qualify for a mortgage immediately.

There are several different categories of people that we like to work with. First and foremost, ideal clients are those who have enough income to be able to make the payments and pay the mortgage when they buy the house from us in the future. Their credit situation is such that, even if they don't qualify for a traditional mortgage right this minute, within two or three years they will.

Therefore, it's very important for you to become knowledgeable about what the mortgage industry is looking for in a qualified applicant. With the mortgage rules tightening up over recent years and the so-called B lenders no longer lending money to people with less than a perfect credit, a great opportunity has been created for those of us interested in becoming Rent-to-Own investors. As a result, the quality of clients that we get to choose from is much better now than it was four or five years ago!

In a future chapter we'll discuss partnering with a broker and why you need one. When you have a good mortgage broker working with you, he will give you a good understanding of what the mortgage industry requires of its candidates. This way, you can learn to distinguish the good apples from the bad; in other words, those who don't fit the mortgage criteria right now but likely will within a year, two or three. And, by the same token, you'll be able to recognize those who won't ever get a mortgage, so you don't waste your time dealing with them.

Client Category # 1: "Cash-Only" Consumers

There are many examples of people with whom the conventional lending community is not willing to work. Since the lenders tend to focus on a person's credit history rather than on his present financial situation, a lot of people who have never had credit problems, and who have always paid cash for everything, do not qualify for a mortgage.

In reality, these folks have decent jobs and incomes, and are very good with their money. They have the "save up to buy later" mind set rather than the "borrow to buy now", much like people of our grandparents' generation (when credit was not so easily available). They don't have credit card debt, because they don't use credit cards. They don't have vehicle loans, because they pay cash for their cars and trucks. They are very responsible with their money and they hate the idea of having a debt. You'd think these people would get rewarded for that good behaviour but they don't.

When they decide that it is time to purchase a home, they run up against a big problem. It's pretty tough to save enough cash to purchase a $250,000 - $300,000 home! And this is when they realize that they will have to get a loan to buy a property. They start applying for mortgages, and they are surprised when they cannot get one (no matter what kind of income they have).

Actually, if you look at them from the bank's point of view, it makes sense. They have zero credit history. They don't have any evidence of making loan payments on time because they've always paid cash for everything. They have no history of having borrowed money from anyone anywhere else. So, the banks have no criteria by which to measure them for credit worthiness. Unless they have a lot of collateral, they aren't going to qualify for a mortgage.

Client Category # 2: New Canadians

Then, we have new Canadians – immigrants who might have been very successful in their countries of origin, but credit-reporting systems usually don't transfer from one country to another. A person like that could land in Canada, have a good job and enough money for a down payment for a home, but he would have no established credit. Until this person develops a track record that the banks can look at and say he is reliable in repaying money, he won't get qualified for a mortgage.

As an aside, we can certainly empathize with these new arrivals. I lived overseas for many years so I have a unique perspective and can appreciate this situation both as a Canadian who once was an immigrant getting started in a new country, as well as someone who moved back to this country. In fact, when I came back to Canada, my situation was very similar to that of a brand new immigrant, as I had no established credit history either! The banks wouldn't give me a mortgage because I had no "track record" with them.

As these immigrants often come from poorer nations, they're grateful for the second chance and thrilled to live the Canadian dream. To be quite frank, they often become much more successful than native-born Canadians because they've got more gumption, motivation and ambition. They tend to be hard workers, movers and shakers, and are willing to do whatever it takes to create their own "Canadian Dream Life". Even when they realize that they don't qualify for a mortgage, they remain positive that one day in the future they'll own a home. And quite often they've brought money with them from their country that they can use as an option deposit. So, these highly motivated, hard-working people who are willing to do whatever it takes to eventually qualify for a traditional mortgage, certainly fall into the category of ideal clients.

Also, as they have no credit history, they don't have anything negative in their past that would stop them from building their credit. They're one of the easiest groups to establish good quality credit in a fairly short period of time because they don't have any skeletons in their closets that would haunt them when it comes time to apply for a mortgage. For all these reasons, if you have an opportunity to work with this calibre of new Canadians, it is quite easy to get them qualified for a mortgage within the time frame of your Rent-to-Own program.

The only challenge of working with immigrants could be the language barrier. In that case, you must make sure the client understands all of your paperwork completely. You might have to bring in someone who speaks their language perfectly, and who also speaks English very, very well to explain the paperwork to him step-by-step before he signs on the dotted line. Also, you should suggest to him that he gets his own independent legal advice, so that all the bases are covered and there are no misunderstandings of any kind.

Here's the bottom line: People without established credit are one of the best groups to work with (whether they're new Canadians or cash-only consumers).

Client Category # 3: Self-Employed

Another important category of people we work with is self-employed individuals. This is another excellent group of potential clients because banks don't really like lending money to people who run their own businesses. Why? Mostly because of the likelihood of failure – as many as 80% of all new businesses don't make it to the five- year mark and a large chunk of them go under within the first two years of their existence. So, unless a self-employed individual has at least two years of tax returns showing a high enough income to be able to afford the property he wants to purchase, the banks won't touch him with a 10-foot pole.

This holds especially true for start-ups, because it takes a few years for a business to be up and running and turning a healthy profit. Even if a person has a good cash flow, due to start-up costs and other expenses inherent to a new business, his net income may not be high enough or steady enough to satisfy risk-averse lending institutions.

What you will also come across when working with self-employed people is that they have been "creatively" minimizing their income. They have paid many of their personal expenses from the company (also known as "business write-offs"). This is a smart tax-savings strategy, and is one of the main perks of being a small business owner. However, it comes around to bite them in the derriere when they want to get a mortgage. They cannot prove their true income to the bank's satisfaction, so they either won't qualify for a mortgage at all, or not for one that's sufficient to buy the house they want.

This is where you swoop in like a good house fairy. If you see that you're dealing with a self-employed person whose expenses are not likely to continue at high a level (or who can begin to show his "true" income for the bank), and that within a year or two he would qualify for a conventional mortgage, he is an ideal client. If his business is doing well, he will want a better / more expensive home because he has the cash flow to afford that. And since no bank will give him mortgage, a R2O is like manna from heaven to him.

Client Category # 4: New Professionals

The fourth category of clients we like to work with are new high-income professionals – dentists, lawyers, doctors, chiropractors, architects, etc. When they're starting just fresh out of university, many of them have a huge student loan debt hanging over their heads, which throws off their financial lives just as they're getting established.

These people won't qualify for a mortgage with the picky Big Banks either, although their problem is not due to a poor credit rating. While they have enough income to pay off their loans and other debts they have incurred while studying, their total debt ratio of loan payments to income does not fit the bank's criteria. Once you see that their income is going up and their loan payments are decreasing, you know that within a couple of years they will qualify for a mortgage. So that's another "ideal client" category right there.

So far, we looked at cash-only consumers, new Canadians, self-employed business people, as well as new professionals. Our fifth and probably the biggest category are folks who, for one reason or another, have damaged credit. It is from this category that most of our Rent-to-Own clients come from.

Client Category # 5: Damaged Credit

Mostly, these are good, hard-working people who, often through no fault of their own, experience some life-altering event that temporarily messes up their credit. It could be that the recession did away with their once high-paying jobs. Maybe they had health problems, suffered a setback such as a temporary unemployment, or perhaps one spouse in a two-income family lost his or her job and they could no longer pay all their bills. It could also be someone who blew all his money on expensive cars or other purchases. Any number of factors, even if temporary, could damage a person's credit enough for them not to qualify for a mortgage.

Even after they get new jobs, solve their problems, pay their bills, and become financially solvent again, it still takes time to re-establish good credit. Until that happens, the banks will refuse to lend to them.

A lot of people fit into this particular category. They got into financial trouble due to tragic events described above, irresponsible and dumb spending habits, and/or poor financial planning and management in the past. Whatever the reasons, their credit took a beating.

Hopefully, with time, these people will draw valuable lessons from their experience. They will realize how difficult it is to live with damaged credit, and become more responsible about their finances. Once that happens and they straighten themselves out, they will qualify for a mortgage sometime down the road.

From our perspective they have a good job. They're ready to turn things around. They want to get into their own house, but the banks won't deal with them.

You may be wondering just about now how we can trust these people enough to enter into a R2O deal with them. After all, they have demonstrated poor judgment and bad spending habits in the past.

We ask that these folks put in some serious cash up front, so that they have their own skin in the game. The more money they put up front when we begin the process of getting them into a R2O home, the more comfortable we feel.

If you're feeling kind of iffy about a potential client, especially someone who you know has a spotty credit history from financial mismanagement, ask him to come up with a lot more cash as your non-refundable option deposit than you normally would. If they cannot or will not do that, then don't do business with them. It's that simple.

This is not a perfect world, and from time to time, you'll run into people who don't inspire confidence in you. If you feel that a potential client needs to prove to you he is serious and committed, feel free to ask for a bigger sum of money up front.

Always look at it from a "worst-case scenario" viewpoint. If the worst happens and the client backs out of the deal, with that big non-refundable option deposit you insisted on up front, you have a financial cushion to last you a few months while you find another person for that property. You can Rent-to-Own it to someone else, and still have a very good deal.

By the way, in the Hot Tip section of this chapter, we'll talk about bankruptcies versus consumer proposals, so you can learn to differentiate between the two as they pertain to your potential clients.

Okay, so in conclusion, there are all sorts of folks who don't qualify for a mortgage right now, but will in the future. These are the kind of people we like to deal with, and we refer to them as our ideal clients: New Canadians, self-employed people, new professionals, and even those who had financial difficulties in the past but now have a promising future. One thing they all have in common is that they can't get a conventional mortgage due to poor (or no) credit.

As long as they can prove to us that they have sufficient income to qualify for a mortgage in two or three years, and as long as they're able to live up to their commitments outlined in the R2O agreement (up-front payment, higher than normal rent, maintenance of the house, buying the property from us at the end of the agreed-upon time period at a pre-defined price), we'll all come out as winners.

In the next chapter we're going to talk about the Rent-to-Own process with our client's choice method.

Hot Tip: The Difference Between Bankruptcy and Consumer Proposal

There are all sorts of damaged credit scenarios. At what point do we look at consumer proposal people and bankruptcy people?

You'll learn more about credit and credit repair in one of our later chapters.

Believe it or not, we actually like to work with people who have gone through bankruptcy because, like those with bad credit, they now have a clean slate. Once they're discharged from their bankruptcy, if they have a little guidance and a little track to run on, they can repair their credit remarkably quickly, and they become excellent candidates for our Rent-to-Own program, even more so than people who have blemished credits and are still carrying a fair amount of consumer debt that they have to deal with in addition to trying to save up for a down payment or pay a premium rent. People with bankruptcy don't have consumer debt payments so they can earmark their entire income towards becoming homeowners, and that makes them excellent candidates for us, even though the banks are not willing to deal with them at this point.

By the way, there is a difference between bankruptcy and a consumer proposal. A bankruptcy is essentially wiping off all the debts the person has.

Related to that is either an informal or a formal consumer proposal, which is basically making an arrangement with your debtors to accept a lesser amount or stop charging interest on your debt. You will pay off the loans (or a significant portion of the loans) over a period of time. This can take anywhere from two to five years.

The problem with consumer proposals is that, at the end of the day, you have to pay off your debts, which you wouldn't have to do in a bankruptcy proceeding. And while you're making payments, your credit is totally shot.

This means that you're not rebuilding your credit the way you would be if you had been discharged from bankruptcy. So although it seems like you should be rewarded for diligently paying back a significant portion of your debts, for the purposes of credit, it is actually worse than bankruptcy (even though bankruptcy carries somewhat of a stigma with it). Your credit won't start rebuilding until you've finished the proposal, which could be three or four years. During that time, we won't be able to get you re-established for a mortgage.

So if you are dealing with people in the midst of a bankruptcy (not yet discharged), or still in the process of paying off their credit proposal, remember that the "clean slate" starting point for repairing their credit has not yet begun.

The "credit repair clock" only starts ticking for them once the bankruptcy has been formally discharged or once the credit report has been properly finalized.

You can still work with these people prior to the finalization of their situation, but be sure to plan out the length of the R2O term accordingly.

CHAPTER 6

THE CLIENT'S CHOICE 10 STEP R2O FORMULA

As the title suggests, in this chapter we're going to talk about the whole process, from start to finish, in a "client's choice" Rent-to-Own deal. There are 10 basic steps.

Step One: Get Your Finances Organized

The first thing you should do is ensure that your financing is in place ahead of time. You may choose to work with an investor. In this case, you don't have to come up with any money out of your own pocket. But for the sake of this example, let's assume you're doing the deal alone, using your own money.

First of all, you have to know that you're buying the rental property under the new mortgage rules. This means you have to put 20% down. Before you even start the process, find out what the average price for the starter home is in your area. Then calculate 20% of that for down payment, plus money for closing costs (about 2%, as already mentioned in Chapter 4). Check your own credit. Find a mortgage broker and get pre-qualified for the purchase of an investment property ahead of time. (Of course, all this is based on your own credit and ability to qualify for a mortgage). Have your down payment and closing money lined up, whether from equity in a home that you already own or from whatever source you're choosing to use.

Fill out the mortgage paperwork and get all of the documentation needed to get pre-qualified to buy this home. It sounds simple, doesn't it? But it can sometimes be a bit of a process, especially now that parameters, rules and regulations for getting a mortgage for an investment property have been tightened up. If you're new to this game, you may not know what paperwork you'll need. Basically, it's the contract to purchase and then sell the house. If you're working with a real estate agent, he or she will help you with all that. Even so, you'd be wise to show the paperwork to a lawyer (especially one specializing in real estate transactions), just to make sure everything is in order.

Step Two: Get Your Legal Paperwork Organized

Chapter Ten is all about the legal paperwork needed for R2O deals. But in a nutshell, one of the things that can go wrong with

Rent-to-Own programs is people not having a good, clear contract in place, and that can generate disputes. So you need to work with a lawyer on what we call an option agreement, which is the agreement where you give your client the right to buy the home from you within a certain time at a certain price, and under certain conditions (up-front payment, rent credits, maintenance, etc.). You're going to need a lease agreement and an option to purchase agreement. If you're working with another investor who's putting up his money into this deal, you're also going to need a lease agreement, an option agreement, and a contract of purchase and sale. That's the main documentation you'll need and all that has to be outlined in clear, legally binding English. You want to have this entire paperwork ready before you start talking to clients.

By the way, we'll talk about lawyers as part of your power team in the next chapter.

After you have pre-qualified for a mortgage, have all your legal paperwork ready, arranged the financing, and know what price range of properties is available to you, you can start marketing for clients. That too will be covered in a future chapter, which will provide guidance on marketing, choosing a suitable client, pre-qualifying him, and all the related topics.

Step Three: Finding and Qualifying Your Clients

Once you have your marketing in place and start taking applications, you will have to talk to a lot of people to find the gem of a client that is the right fit for your program. Unlike renting, the candidates for this program are going to be those who don't qualify for a mortgage now but, as you can ascertain with the help of your credit specialist, will be in a position to qualify within two or three years (which is when your program is designed to be completed). So you really have to turn over a lot of stones and kiss a lot of frogs to find the ideal client for your R2O deal. Again, we will explain exactly how to pre-qualify clients in a later chapter in this book.

Let's say that you have found a client who fits your parameters. He has enough cash to cover all the costs, which, as we already stated several times, consist of up-front non-refundable deposit, premium rent, maintenance, and utilities. The next step is fun, especially for the client: He is going to shop for the home of his dreams!

Step Four: Go House Shopping!

In a deal like this, we use realtors with whom we have worked before. They know ahead of time the price range the client qualified for. They usually look at quite a few houses before the client finds the one he really likes, and then narrows the search down to three choices. Once that is done, we look at the top contender and make sure it's within the ballpark of the price range we established. If everything looks good, then we make an offer to purchase that property.

That's how we do the "client's choice" R2O. However, when you talk about the Rent-to-Own concept to a potential client, he doesn't usually think in terms of picking out his dream home himself. He thinks you, the landlord, will line up a property for him. But at the end of the day, this is going to be his house, so it's important that he decides what he would like to eventually own. You're the good guy here, a hero of sorts, because you make it possible for this person (with whom banks won't work) to own his ideal home faster than he would ever be able to on his own.

This is not to say that we don't set certain conditions on what kind of properties we're willing to purchase. These parameters include the price range that the client can afford, based on his income, debt ratio, etc. Therefore, his aspirations should be realistic, not just wishful thinking.

One of several types of properties we shy away from is rural houses. Some clients might dream about life on a farm, but we, as investors, are not keen on it. The reason for this is that if the deal doesn't go through, we'll be stuck with a house that other people might not want; after all, living in remote rural areas is not everyone's cup of tea. Searching for a client who wants that kind of property is like looking for a needle in a haystack – no pun intended. We certainly don't want to end up "sitting on" a house that no other client will want.

Just like we stay away from rural properties and farmhouses, we don't want homes in teenie- weenie communities or one-industry towns, where there's not much going on in real estate. It's all about smart exit strategies, in case Murphy's Law strikes and the client reneges on the deal.

Yet another type of property that we avoid is the mobile home in mobile home parks. Those properties are more rental material. Finding a client for a mobile home in a mobile home park where there's a PAD fee, and the actual home itself isn't worth all that much, is not a given. So you won't see us working with this type of property.

Even mobile homes sitting on their own land can be problematic. If they're older, a lot of banks won't put mortgages on them. In fact, banks won't touch most mobile homes unless they have basements or permanent foundations. So it would be crazy to take on a piece of property that wouldn't qualify for a conventional mortgage.

Another property that we stay clear of is a fixer-upper. If someone wants to buy a house that needs $50,000 worth of repairs to be marketable, he'd better have that $50,000 up front, because if something doesn't work out with the client and we end up being stuck with this ruin, we won't be able to put someone else in it or resell it. This is not to say that there aren't lots of people out there who'd love to buy a fixer-upper and remodel it themselves. We're not saying this is bad. All we're saying is that we don't like and won't purchase this kind of property ourselves. If the client wants to add some value to the house, build a new deck, update it, or whatever, that's great. We're all for it. But the house has to be structurally sound and in a good condition to begin with, not a dilapidated shack that needs significant repairs requiring a lot of money. Thanks, but no thanks.

Here's the bottom line: We're doing the R2O program to make money. In a business sense, the numbers have to make sense to us. We buy property for a given price and intend to sell it at a profit at the end of the program. So it's logical that we're only interested in properties that will appreciate in value and are therefore a good investment. Farmhouses aren't, and neither are mobile homes or fixer-uppers. We feel much more comfortable with traditional single-family homes, half duplexes, condos, town houses, and such – nice starter homes in a good condition and in good neighbourhoods.

OK, back to our regularly scheduled topic!

Step Five: Make the Offer!

Now, let's assume the client has found the house he likes. We've checked it out on MLS and taken a look at it. If the property meets all our criteria, we put an offer on it. Here's a nice thing: We don't have to bargain with the seller and try to get a "steal of a deal." If needed, we can pay fair market price for the house. We don't want to pay too much for it, but we don't have to bargain too hard and lose a deal either. However, how we make the offer and what we include in it is very important.

We go through all the standard steps that anybody would use when purchasing a home. We make it subject to financing, a lawyer's approval of the documentation, and a satisfactory inspection.

Step Six: Inspect the Home

This step is very important. This is where you want your client to be involved because he's the one who'll ultimately own the house. That's why he should be present during the inspection so he's informed of what little flaws there are (and virtually every house has some). If the client is not present during the inspection, he can come back to you two years later and say "Oh, I wasn't aware of this problem at the time of the purchase." On the other hand, if the client knows what's going on with the house, has an opportunity to discuss any findings with the inspector, and still wants to purchase the property, warts and all, then he can't blame you later or say he was unaware of any problems. If the property is satisfactory to him at the time of the initial purchase, it should also be satisfactory two years later, or whenever he buys it from you.

Speaking about the inspection, there's a little trick we do if we're trying to get the price of the house down – an advanced negotiation strategy. Here is how this works: You make an offer that's very close to the asking price. If the home is in a slower market, the seller is absolutely thrilled to have a solid offer on the table from a serious investor. He considers it a done deal. But if the inspection reveals problems with the house, you can go back and renegotiate either the price or the terms of the purchase.

For example, if it turns out that the furnace is on its last legs, one of the conditions we renegotiate is that the owners either replace the furnace or reduce the price to make it worth our while to buy and install a new one ourselves. So whatever's not right with the house, even if it's relatively minor, you can use it as a reason to lower the purchase price of the home.

Step Seven: Making SURE Your Client is Committed

OK, by now you are well on your way to making this deal fly! Congratulations! But before you consider it to be a "slam dunk," you have to make sure your client is truly on board for the duration of the deal. This is the last chance for you to get out of buying the home, relatively unscathed. So if the client has cold feet, this is the time to know it!

Before you move ahead any further, make sure the client has:

a. signed off on an official agreement to work with you.
b. given you the FULL option deposit.
c. reviewed and signed the lease and option agreement (and preferably gone over it with his own lawyer).

If he changes his mind at this point, you can still back out of the deal and not suffer any serious financial loss.

Usually everything is fine, and now you can move on to step eight.

Step Eight: Buying the House

Now, let's assume that the inspection went well, the house is good, and you're getting it at fair market value. Your next step is closing on the property. This is quite a simple process because the realtor does most of the work, and it goes through your mortgage broker and your lawyer. Everybody's signing off on paperwork. Title is getting checked – that's a very important step because you want to make sure there won't be any nasty surprises associated with the property that will bite you in the ass somewhere down the road. That's one more reason to work with an experienced real estate lawyer who'll be looking out for your best interests.

Step Nine: Moving the Client In, and Helping Him Qualify for a Mortgage

Okay, now the house is purchased. Your client signed a lease and an option to purchase the property by a pre-determined date. You received your entire non-refundable deposit. By now, it's a done deal.

Let's look again at the numbers we have in a previous chapter. We purchased a $250,000 home and we use 80 basis points of the value. That works out to $2,000 a month, of which 20% ($400 a month) will be given back to the client as rent credits once he successfully purchases the home at the agreed price. You'll see that in our spreadsheet and calculations, where we use 80 basis points to establish our monthly rent payment.

Now the client is in the home he picked. He's thrilled. Everything is going well: He paid an option deposit, which will be applied towards his down payment when he purchases the property. He's paying above-average market rent, a portion of which is being credited towards the purchase price. Again, part of this whole lease agreement is that he's responsible for maintenance on the property, as well as all the utility bills. For you, this is a very hands-off type of investment. Basically, you're just sitting around waiting until the client has to buy this house from you so you can get additional money on top of what you've already got out of this deal. However, there's one important thing you should be doing during this process: Keep an ongoing contact with your client to make sure that he's doing what he must to get financing when it's time for him to buy the property. That's called credit counselling. We'll have a chapter on that in this book as well.

Very briefly, this process focuses on making sure the client will qualify for a mortgage when the time comes to buy the house from you. Together with your mortgage person or credit counsellor you're going over the steps the client will have to take in order to be able to get a mortgage in the two or three year time period. So before you even start looking for a house, you must discuss those steps with the client so he knows it's a requirement, a condition of the deal. It's basically your credit repair plan. The client has to agree to those conditions, otherwise the deal is off.

Frankly, we don't see why any serious candidate for the house would scoff at credit counselling. After all, he sees the advantages of this type of R2O program, which is very beneficial to him. As for us, the investors, we don't really want to be turning around and trying to find other clients for this property. So, we're doing everything we can to help him purchase it.

Our goal is 100% success rate. Realistically speaking, and human nature being what it is, that's probably not going to happen, but we're doing everything we reasonably can to get as close as possible to that 100% success rate: We've given our client guidance. We've hooked him up with a credit counsellor or a mortgage person to explain all the things that he needs to do. He has agreed to those terms and he must live up to the agreement. Once we buy the house, we've kept our part of the bargain. Be aware however, that this is our way of doing business. There are other Rent-to-Own programs available that operate differently and not as thoroughly: These investors don't have the knowledge about credit and don't give a credit repair plan to their clients. In those cases, success rate is, not surprisingly, much lower than ours. If these so-called investors don't guide their clients on an on-going basis from beginning to end, what other outcome can they expect?

But we're trying to focus on the positive aspects and results of the client's choice R2O. We've seen this happen time and again – if everything goes smoothly (as it does in most cases for us and our clients), this is a very rewarding experience for all concerned. Yes, we get some cash out of it at the end, but we also get the satisfaction of having helped a deserving family get into the starter home of their dreams, which they wouldn't have been able to achieve any other way. That's a fantastic feeling. And for the clients, it's just as, if not more, rewarding: They have their initial option deposit, which applies towards their down payment. They have their rental credits that go towards their down payment as well. In the example of the $250,000 home, they have almost $20,000 paid in towards a $275,000 home at the end of two or three years.

Step Ten: CASH-OUT (Sell the House to the Client)

That's the beauty of the "Client's Choice" R2O process. By the end of two or three years, everything falls into place. We've helped clients repair their credit. They've been in contact with a mortgage person. You really can't put a dollar value on the enjoyment you get out of helping someone become a homeowner with your help, guidance and expertise. You certainly can't get that from being a "normal" income property landlord because, although you're providing a roof over their heads and a fair arrangement, you don't help them achieve a goal, a dream.

Let's have another look over the things we covered in this chapter. This is our 10-step client's choice R2O process:

Arrange your financing ahead of time. Make sure that you have the money in place and the mortgage approved before you start looking for clients and houses.

Make sure that you have all your legal paperwork looked over by your lawyer ahead of time.

Find a pre-qualified client. This is someone who doesn't qualify to purchase a home traditionally right now, but will within the next two to three years. He has some cash up front to get involved in the game.

Once you have him pre-selected and pre-qualified, send him shopping for a home with a friendly realtor.

If the house he selects meets your parameters, make an offer on it. After you've made the offer and before the deal closes, it's important that your client shows the option agreement and the lease to an independent legal counsel so the client fully understands his obligations and rights under this program. (See Hot Tip, below)

Get the inspection done. That might be a good opportunity to renegotiate the price a little bit if you come up with some problems. If that strategy doesn't work out to your satisfaction, walk away from the deal and tell the client to look for another property.

Have the lease and the option ready for the client.

If everything looks good, close on the deal and buy the property.

Help your client with credit counselling and on-going monitoring to make sure he qualifies for a mortgage when the R2O program comes to an end.

Sell the house to the client and cash out at the end.

In the next chapter, we're going to talk about how to create your "R2O Dream Team".

Hot Tip 1:

As mentioned above, you should encourage your client to show the paperwork to his own legal counsel: The lease, the option agreement, payment schedule, amounts he'll pay and credits he'll receive at the end of the program, as well as all the other details. This is especially important if English is not the client's mother tongue and he may have difficulty understanding everything that's outlined in the documents.

If he declines, you should have him sign an additional paper stating that you encouraged him to get legal counsel and he chose not to do so out of his own volition. This way, if anything should go wrong, or if he claims he was not aware of this or that, you're protected.

Hot Tip 2: How Much to Pay for a Property?

With the client's choice R2O method, you can comfortably pay fair market price for a home. When you are making an offer on a home, be sure that your realtor has pulled up the "comps" (comparables) and that you have a good idea of the true market value of the property. You should check the assessed value from the most recent property tax assessment as well. Compare the asking price with the "normal" variance from tax assessments for other properties in the area. Your realtor should be able to help you.

Here's what we do: We find out what "fair market price" is, and we try to pay $3,000 to $5,000 less than that. If the offer is accepted, then the "discount" we received is usually enough to cover the closing costs, property transfer taxes, and other costs involved in buying the property.

Why do we do this? Because this way our TOTAL starting price is very close to what true market value is, and the "future price" we'll charge our client will more likely be in line with true market values at that time. This means that it will be easier to get the house appraised for the asking price, and to get our client financing to purchase it.

Chapter 7

Your R20 Dream Team

As you could see in previous chapters, if you want to succeed in the R2O business, you simply cannot go it alone. You need the help of a select group of professionals to make the whole process work well. Sure, you're the dealmaker here and you're in control, but that doesn't mean you shouldn't surround yourself with people who have the expertise that you may not have yourself. You need these folks to pull it all together for you.

In this chapter, we're going to talk about your R2O "Dream Team" or "Power Team" (as some call it), who should be on it and why. The sooner you get this group organized, start communicating with them and explaining your business plan, the better it will be.

Let's begin with your friendly mortgage broker.

Mortgage Broker

We prefer to work with mortgage brokers rather than directly with banks because when they place a mortgage with a bank or another lender, they'll get paid a commission by the company that provided a mortgage, not by you. In other words, it doesn't cost you anything. They'll get you equal or better rates than what you can get from the bank. Plus, they're motivated to make sure that you get a mortgage, because if you don't, they won't get paid. They'll be honest with you and let you know what you have to do in order to obtain a mortgage.

Another benefit of working with an independent mortgage broker is that he has access to multiple lenders, while a bank can only offer you its own products, which are limited. A mortgage broker, on the other hand, can work with all the major banks plus all the other lenders as well. Yet another huge benefit of partnering with a good mortgage broker is that he can also be a source for clients for you. Quite often, clients come into his office wanting to get pre-qualified for a mortgage but don't qualify right now. As a matter of fact, our best clients were referred to us by our mortgage brokers – people who had the income and money available for a down payment, but, for whatever reason, did not qualify for a conventional mortgage. So that's another thing you want to be talking about with your mortgage broker.

You may be wondering where you can find this gem of a broker. If your community has a real estate investment group, it would be beneficial for you to join and ask other members for recommendations of brokers who fit your criteria; in other words, those who have experience working with real estate investors. Even in this day and age of Internet and other technologies, word of mouth and personal recommendations are still the best ways to find a reliable team member.

Interview candidates, talk with different mortgage brokers, and don't necessarily settle for the first one you visit. We certainly didn't. We looked around and found one who was creative enough to get deals done, and we're still using this broker today.

So now you found a great mortgage broker. Before you embark on a R2O deal, you need to determine what kind of property (price range) you're eligible for. While you're in this process, it's good to have a long discussion with the mortgage broker about what exactly the process involves – what criteria they require in order to qualify someone for a mortgage, what credit scores are all about, how they work, what ratios are, how debt service ratios work, and what numbers the mortgage people are looking for. As you can see, there's a lot of ground to cover and you should not only ask the mortgage broker what you're qualified for, but also what process lenders go through to determine what you qualify for.

As we mentioned before, if you're just getting into this business, ideally you should be the investor in your first couple of deals. You shouldn't immediately be trying to get other people's money without putting a little bit of your own skin in the game and getting your Rent-to-Own business rolling that way. But some people also have the idea that they want to buy multiple properties themselves. If that's your case, you should have the conversation with your mortgage broker right off the bat and let him know that you plan to buy several properties. Most mortgage brokers are not accustomed to working with investors. They're only used to working with people buying their own homes (or perhaps one additional property). If you're planning to buy five, six, seven, or eight properties in your own name, then you definitely have to make sure that you get it set up properly from the get go.

That's even more important because recent changes in mortgage rules impact real estate investors more than anyone else. If your mortgage broker has no experience with investors, he or she may not have a full understanding of the effect of the new rules, and how you should have a plan in place as to which lenders you'll be working with when buying multiple investment properties. That's why, when choosing a mortgage broker, you should make sure he has ample experience working with investors with multiple properties.

Another thing you should explain very clearly to your mortgage broker is that you might become one of his best customers because each deal that you do is potentially two deals for your mortgage broker. In fact, ask him to read this book so he understands what your goal is. He'll get a commission when you or your investors initially buy the property. Then he'll get another commission when your client buys the property because chances are you will encourage the client to use the same mortgage broker to purchase the house from you at the end of the program.

In the meantime, the broker is going to be working with the client, helping him with credit counselling to get qualified for a mortgage when his R2O term finishes.

As you can see, an experienced mortgage broker is a very important part of your power team, so choose wisely.

Real Estate Lawyer

Another person on whom you'll rely for all your transactions is a good real estate lawyer. We already partly covered his role in Chapter 6, but let's elaborate further.

One of the keys to success of your R2O program are contracts that outline your responsibilities as well as the clients' rights and obligations in a clear manner, leaving no room for misunderstandings or misinterpretations.

Later on we'll show you where to get sample templates that you can show to your lawyer, so he or she can confirm that the wording is correct and legally binding. If you want to change or personalize any part of it to fit your own specific needs and requirements, make sure the lawyer approves it.

We want to emphasize again that ideally you should be dealing with an experienced real estate attorney, not a jack-of-all-trades who dabbles in all areas of the law but specializes in none. Of course, if you live in a really small town, you may not have the option of working with a real estate lawyer, but it will certainly be worth your while if you can find one in a next town, even if it involves some travel.

How do you go about finding a good real estate attorney? Here, too, word of mouth and personal referrals are most effective. You can ask your mortgage broker – he has probably worked with several so can recommend the best one. Also, the real estate investment club (which you hopefully have joined by now) may have good leads.

Some criteria you should adhere to:

1. Don't choose someone who is the cheapest. Yes, you want competitive and reasonable pricing, but if someone offers you rates that are suspiciously low, there's probably a reason for that. Steer away from that person; you certainly don't want to stick around long enough to find out why he's so cheap.
2. Try to find a lawyer who is also a real estate investor himself because he will actually have hands-on experience and money in the game, so he knows all the ropes. True, legal experts who are also real estate investors are not necessarily easy to find, but if you do, they'll be your best bet. If not, at least go with a lawyer who has an in-depth knowledge of the field.

Before you hire an attorney, interview him and get a sense of his expertise and personality. You want to work with someone you feel comfortable with, especially since you'll be dealing with him on a regular, on-going basis.

Real Estate Agent

Okay, on to the next member of your team – the real estate agent. He is important for several reasons, not the least of which is that he'll help you find your ideal clients and pre-qualify them. Once that step is done, the agent will line up the houses and show them to the clients. Then, he will take all the necessary steps toward purchasing that property for you and, at the end of the program, selling it to the clients. It goes without saying (but we'll say it anyway) that you want an agent who has hopefully worked with investors before, has experience with multiple purchases, closings, and all of the things that are associated with your R2O program.

As we discussed earlier, the real estate business has a high turnover. If you want to develop a long-term relationship with a realtor, you should be looking for someone who has been in the business for a number of years rather than a newbie. He or she might be here today but gone tomorrow and then you'll have to start all over again, looking for someone else who meets your requirements.

Having said that, we hasten to add that there's another, perfectly good way of integrating a rookie realtor into your team. Some people (including ourselves) have actually worked with two different realtors at the same time, an experienced one and a newbie. The advantage of the newbie is that he or she is hungry, motivated, eager and trainable to boot. Because that person is just starting out in the business and trying to establish a clientele, he might be more willing to bend backwards and do whatever you ask. The more experienced realtor, on the other hand, might be more set in his ways and used to doing things his own way. There are two schools of thought on that. It's up to you to decide which one you prefer.

Whichever scenario you go with, the important thing when dealing with a real estate agent is to make sure you and he are on the same page; that he knows what your business goals are and what you're trying to accomplish. He should align himself to your expectations and not try to cut corners. For example, you definitely don't want him telling your clients behind your back that they can get qualified for a mortgage on their own when they don't have the faintest clue how to do this.

You must give him clear guidelines on what price range of properties, and neighbourhoods to show or not to show the clients – no rural houses, mobile park homes, fixer-uppers and such. If the clients are interested in a house that's not suitable for the program, the agent should steer them towards a more appropriate property and not push you to change your parameters. It's important that he understands you're the boss and he works for you, not for the clients. You don't want the realtor to get too emotionally attached or too chummy with the clients. Bottom line is: The agent's priority should be your best interests. It's as simple as that.

Where can you find a good real estate agent? Again, personal referrals and your investment club buddies. And, if you already have a mortgage broker and a lawyer lined up, more than likely they'll be able to recommend some realtors. It's up to you to vet them.

Home Inspector

The fourth member of your team is the home inspector. He is essential to our program because, as investors, we want to do all we can to avoid buying problematic properties. We're only interested in good, solid homes with the least amount of maintenance headaches – houses that are going to be good value for our clients, for us, as well as for our investors (if we have any).

You may find that home inspection is quite expensive, but you should never skimp on that. The results of a home inspection can either make or break your deal, so at the end of the day, it's a very good investment.

Again, this is another area where not all home inspectors are created equal. If you live in British Columbia, you are familiar with properties that serve as marijuana growing operations (or "grow ops" as they are called). In that case, your home inspector's top priority should be to determine whether or not the property is now or has ever been a grow operation. Beware that insurance companies won't touch this type of house with a 10-foot pole.

This is just one of the reasons why an experienced home inspector is a must. Even if the property is not a grow operation, it may have other major structural or mechanical flaws – asbestos, radon gas, lead paint, toxic mould, pest infestation, whatever. Basically, a home inspector will give you an informed and impartial opinion on the shape and condition of the house, so you're sure you're not buying a lemon.

Since home inspection is a highly specialized field, you want to pick someone who's knowledgeable, experienced, and trustworthy. Here again, you should ask people in your real estate investors group or your mortgage broker or lawyer to recommend a home inspector. Keep in mind that virtually every house has some minor flaws, but you're looking for anything that could be a significant problem.

We mentioned "experienced" as one of the qualities you should be looking for in a home inspector. We once hired an inspector for a property we were considering buying but that we thought was a bit overpriced. It turned out that the property was in a very good shape and the inspector told that to the sellers! By doing so, the inspector quashed all our chances of negotiating a better price.

A good home inspector should know who he is working for. He should know to keep his mouth shut and only reveal his findings to those who are paying him. All those things that should be common sense – but sometimes aren't – should be discussed when you hire an inspector. Once we had a talk with that particular inspector and explained to him what we were trying to do, he got the message. It has never been a problem since.

Bookkeeper / Accountant

The last, but certainly not the least important member of your team, is a bookkeeper. Whether you're a small business owner or a tycoon, the importance of keeping your financial accounts in order can't be over-emphasized.

Since the R2O program is a business, you must keep this separate from your own personal accounting and tax preparation. The bookkeeper you hire will make sure that you're keeping track of all your income and expenses in a business-like manner. A lot of people don't have a head for numbers (or time to keep the books), so a part-time bookkeeper to keep things organized is a necessity.

Unless your bookkeeper is also a savvy accountant and tax expert, you may need additional help in that regard. You have income from your rent. You have expenses with your mortgage on which only the interest part is tax deductible, as well as your other expenses, such as property taxes and insurance. When you're dealing with properties, you have the closing costs, which you have to keep track of when you're selling the house, so that you know what your capital gain is. All this to say that you need to be working with someone who is knowledgeable, not only in the on-going rental income expenses portion your business, but also the parts that count towards what is called the "adjusted cost base" for the purchase cost and capital gains calculations when you sell the property. That person can also advise you on whether it's worth your while to take depreciation on the property. So yes, a bookkeeper and a tax advisor are a must.

Now that you have your dream / power team in place, it's time to start marketing for clients! Turn the page to Chapter 8.

Hot Tip: Focus On Networking to Build Your "Dream Team"

If you're starting your business from scratch, you would do well to network with other real estate investors. Don't look at them as competitors, but rather as sources of contacts, recommendations, and referrals. If they've been in this business for a while, they likely know reputable mortgage brokers, realtors, lawyers, and other professionals whom you'd want to recruit as members of your team. Networking is like a domino effect. Once you get a recommendation for one person, he or she can then refer you to another, and so on. As a result, your power team will consist of people who have been "road-tested" and come highly recommended by your peers. That's the power of networking, baby!

CHAPTER 8

MARKETING FOR CLIENTS

Since I have background and experience in marketing and Dan is more of a financial wiz, I decided to take a crack at writing this chapter myself and give him some rest.
By Dave Dubeau

Needless to say, clients are the backbone of your business so you have to go all out to attract them – not just anyone, mind you, but the "right" kind of people we described in our "Ideal Client" chapter. Just as a reminder, you'll be looking for people who have a good income and some cash available for the up-front, non-refundable option payment – folks who don't qualify for a mortgage right now, but will in a couple of years.

So how do you go about finding these elusive, ideal rent-to-own clients? There are many ways to do that, so I am going to cover the simplest, easiest to implement and the most effective methods here. Let's call them the "Top 4" R2O Marketing Magnets.

R2O Marketing Magnet # 1: Your R2O WEBSITE

Is it possible to do rent-to-own deals without a website? Yes. But I don't know why you would want to!

Having a good, working website for your R2O business is a HUGE benefit for many reasons:

- It is an amazing time-saver. By having the main information about your program on a website, you can educate your prospective clients 24/7. This saves you an incredible amount of time, since you don't have to explain the same basic things, over and over and over again to people over the phone.
- It is a wonderful pre-qualifier. By explaining what your parameters are for R2O clients, they can see exactly what kind of people you are able to work with, and if they don't fit those criteria, they can eliminate themselves without you having to do it.
- It automates the application process. By having prospective R2O clients fill out their application forms online, you don't have to spend your valuable time doing this on the phone. The completed application is automatically sent to you. You can go over it at your leisure and contact the person at your convenience.
- It gives you a professional image. Now-a-days, if a company does not have a website, it is not perceived as a serious business. By having a decent website, you give yourself credibility in the eyes of your prospective clients.
- It allows you to start connecting with prospects before you actually meet them. By having videos and information about yourself on the site, people will get to know you a bit before they actually meet you. It creates trust and rapport.
- It can be a very inexpensive tool for your business. Getting a basic site set up shouldn't cost you more than a couple of hundred dollars – much less if you do it yourself.

- A website is like having a salesperson working for you, 24/7. Many people are looking for information about rent-to-own programs at very strange times of the day or night. By accessing your website for information, they are able to get it when they want to, and are not limited to contacting you during business hours.
- Once you get your website established, it can also be an online marketing tool to actually attract potential clients to you. If it ends up ranking high in the search engines (like Google, Yahoo, Bing, etc.), it can "organically" bring in people who are interested in your program.

So those are some of the main reasons for having your own website FAST. An important thing to remember is that you do NOT have to do it yourself. You can find a sample website and have a teenager create a similar version for you, and it won't cost you much money.

Please see the sample of my BCRent2Buy.com website:

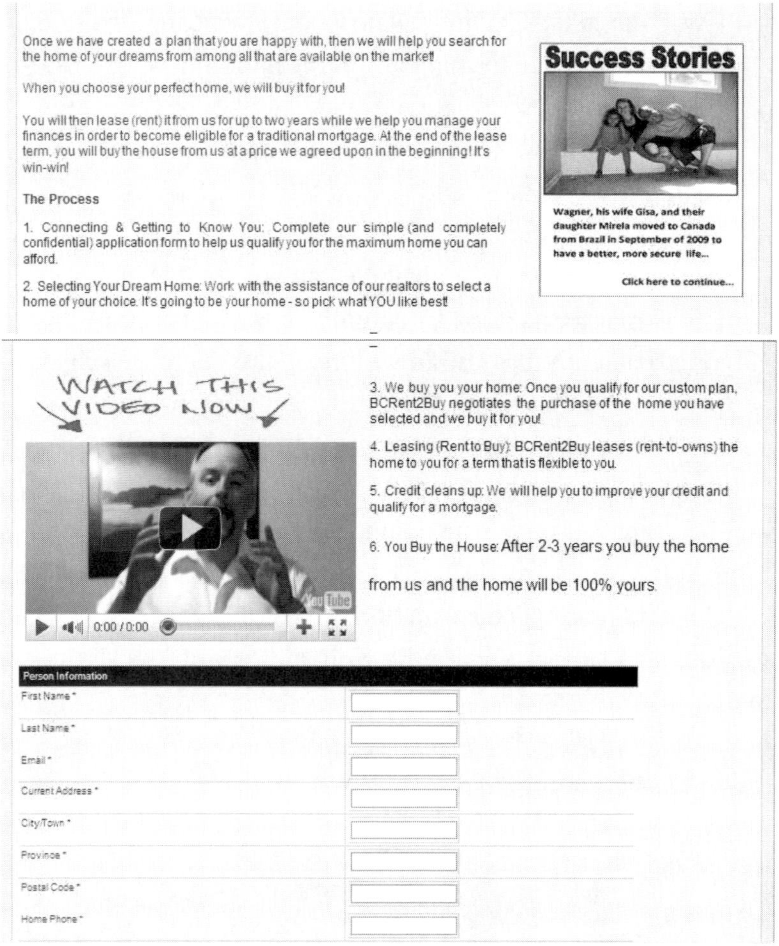

Once we have created a plan that you are happy with, then we will help you search for the home of your dreams from among all that are available on the market!

When you choose your perfect home, we will buy it for you!

You will then lease (rent) it from us for up to two years while we help you manage your finances in order to become eligible for a traditional mortgage. At the end of the lease term, you will buy the house from us at a price we agreed upon in the beginning! It's win-win!

The Process

1. Connecting & Getting to Know You: Complete our simple (and completely confidential) application form to help us qualify you for the maximum home you can afford.

2. Selecting Your Dream Home: Work with the assistance of our realtors to select a home of your choice. It's going to be your home - so pick what YOU like best!

Success Stories

Wagner, his wife Gisa, and their daughter Mirela moved to Canada from Brazil in September of 2009 to have a better, more secure life...

Click here to continue...

WATCH THIS VIDEO NOW

3. We buy you your home: Once you qualify for our custom plan, BCRent2Buy negotiates the purchase of the home you have selected and we buy it for you!

4. Leasing (Rent to Buy): BCRent2Buy leases (rent-to-owns) the home to you for a term that is flexible to you.

5. Credit cleans up: We will help you to improve your credit and qualify for a mortgage.

6. You Buy the House: After 2-3 years you buy the home from us and the home will be 100% yours.

0:00 / 0:00

Person Information

First Name *

Last Name *

Email *

Current Address *

City/Town *

Province *

Postal Code *

Home Phone *

Please notice the following:

1. The use of video throughout. Video is quickly becoming the most popular way of creating content on the web. Many people prefer to watch a video than read a lot of text. Also, with video you are able to connect much better with your potential clients. They get to know you a bit and feel more comfortable working with a "real person" rather than with a faceless company.

2. Some text, but not too much.
3. One main message per page. Try to keep it simple and uncluttered.
4. An online application form at the bottom of each page. Again, my goal with the site is to get as many prospective R2O clients to fill out the application form as possible.
5. The use of SUCCESS STORIES and TESTIMONIALS. Video is absolutely the best, but if you can't get that, then use pictures and written testimonials.

A website is an inexpensive "must-have" in your marketing toolkit if you want to maximize the efficiency and profitability of your R2O business. It does a LOT of the "heavy lifting" for you and saves you a ton of time and effort.

R2O Marketing Magnet # 2:
Your Ideal R2O CLIENT BUSINESS CARD

One quick and simple way of spreading the word and attracting clients is with high-impact, bright-coloured business cards.

The idea is to get them out to as many different places as possible. They're little tent cards so you can stand them up on tables or pin them up on bulletin boards, and since they're in a "loud" colour, they're eye-catching, which is exactly what you want.

First of all, let's go over what NOT to do when you are creating your business card:

Do NOT try to follow the lead of real estate agents, mortgage brokers, etc. and get all excited about plastering your face front and center on your card. Bottom line is this: Nobody really cares what you look like. It is more important to focus on getting your message across than showcasing your face. And let's "face" it, some people (present company excluded, of course) really shouldn't have their headshots on a business card! It will actually cause them to lose potential clients. I know of several people who tried to overcome this by having their pictures "fixed up" a little, or by using their best photo from 1987, when they had hair and weighed 35 pounds less than they do now (ouch...I think I'm talking about myself). The problem is, when you get their business card and compare it with how they look now, it is definitely false advertising!

Do NOT get all worked up and frothy at the mouth about creating a logo for your business, attempting to be all "professional" and creating the perfect "brand" for your new R2O company. I can't tell you how many times I've seen people waste weeks or even months on this crap when they should be out beating the bushes for good real estate deals. Again, nobody really cares about your logo - they just want to know what you can do for them, how you can solve their problem, and get them into a home of their own!

Do NOT try to be cute, stylish or subtle with your business cards. The entire goal of your card is to grab your ideal prospective client's attention FAST and get them to call you...NOW. And if that doesn't work, you want them to keep your card so it will always be a beacon that calls out to them to take ACTION and call you.

Do NOT be the same as everyone else out there. 99% of all business cards are boring, single-sided things with mundane information on them that no one cares about or will remember. I use my tent business cards like a mini-sales letter with as much information as I can on them, so that they will stick out more.

Do NOT go cheap and try to do them yourself on your home printer with the cut-out cards you can get at your local office supply store. Spend a few bucks and get them printed at a real print shop.

So now that I've shared with you what NOT to do, here is what I think you should do: Copy the format of the card I've shown you here!

First of all, make it a BRIGHT (obnoxiously bright) colour. I use eye-catching yellow with black print. I've seen other people use neon orange, neon green, even neon pink!

Remember that the goal is for your card to STICK OUT from the rest. Don't worry that it doesn't look "pretty and professional", the goal is to get your phone to ring, or to get people to go to your website for information.

Secondly, remember that "the more you tell, the more you sell." Use a tent style card where you can fit in a lot of information about your program.

The "first page" of my card is just a BIG, HIGH IMPACT HEADLINE. "Renting SUCKS!" "Rent-to-Own! Kamloops & Area". I also include my website.

The entire goal of the first page is to arouse curiosity and get people to read the inside of the card, where my "mini sales letter" is located.

In my case I write:

We Help Hard-Working Thompson/Okanagan Families to Get Into the Home of their Dreams FAST... Even When the BANKS Say "No".

[I immediately say who my "target market audience" is; in my case, people in the Thompson/Okanagan area. I put in "hard-working" to emphasize that I'm looking for people with jobs (not folks on welfare – as I can't help them). I hit them between the eyes that it is OK if they have been turned down by the banks].

Dear Frustrated Renter:

Does this situation sound familiar? You really want to stop throwing money away on rent and buy your very own home, but the BANKS won't give you a mortgage! Maybe it's because...

- ⊗ You have credit "glitches" from past mistakes.
- ⊗ You have gone through bankruptcy
- ⊗ You are self-employed.
- ⊗ You are a recent immigrant to the country.
- ⊗ You don't have enough credit history.

(Again, I reach out to my target audience: Frustrated Renters. I also describe some of the main categories of people I can work with – those with credit problems, bankruptcy, self-employed folks, etc.).

It doesn't matter what the situation is, if you are a responsible person with a steady income and you want to get into a home of your own, we can probably help you ...FAST !

(I go on to include more pre-qualifying language; in this case, "responsible person with a steady income").

We are not realtors, nor landlords trying to sell a house. We are professional real estate investors based in the Kamloops / Okanagan area and our goal is to help as many local people as possible enjoy all of the benefits of home ownership, even when they have been turned down by the banks.

Our program is simple: You fill out a quick application, and we go over your particular situation. If you like the program, then you find the home you like. With our investors, we BUY the home for you. You rent-to-own the home from us, while we help you get lined up for bank financing. When everything is ready, we transfer title of the home to you! It's now 100% your home! This can save you YEARS of renting and saving.

In the above section, I talk about who we are, what we do, and give people a brief overview of how the program works. I tell enough to whet their appetite for more information, because my entire goal is to get them to contact me.

Finally, I wrap the whole card up with a CALL TO ACTION to go online and fill out our no-obligation application.

The website address is BIG and BOLD, because I would rather have them apply online than call me.

And only at the END do I put in my name and contact information.

On the back page of my card, I summarize the information in easy-to-understand bullet points:

Are you sick and tired of flushing your money down the toilet on rent? Frustrated because you can't get a mortgage?

- Then why not Rent-to-Own your dream home FAST?
- Go through our simple application and orientation.
- Pick out the home that you like the best - you choose it!
- We buy it for you, and you move in!
- You rent-to-own, and we help you get financed to buy.
- We transfer title to you, and it is 100% your own home!

Now you don't have to wait years, save up thousands, and have "perfect" credit to buy a home. We can help you get into the home of your dreams...FAST.

Additional notes about business cards

You will notice that I have my website, BCRent2Buy.com, prominently displayed in bold letters on every side of the business card – the front page, inside page, and the back page. This is because I want to push as many people to my website as I possibly can. That way they can find out more details about the program, pre-qualify themselves some more, and then fill out the online application form. By doing that, I save myself a ton of time and effort, and I automate the process much more.

As you can see, the simple business card can be turned into a very effective marketing tool.

R2O Marketing Magnet # 3: Online Advertising

Just like websites, online advertising is here to stay. So if you are a bit of a technophobe, you'll just have to get used to it!

The good news is this: In our experience, online classified advertising is far less expensive and much more effective than traditional classified advertising in newspapers. In fact, in some cases you can get your ads out for FREE.

Online classified ads offer you the possibility to target only the people you're specifically interested in, not every Tom, Dick and Harry out there. Folks who would like to own a home but can't get a mortgage right now. So online ads allow you to narrow your search to a certain category of people, which is exactly what you want to do.

Another point is that the Internet has killed off a lot of print media. Nearly everyone has a computer, but not everybody buys and reads the newspaper.

Just to give you an example and a ballpark figure, when we advertise on Kijiji in the Halifax area, which has a population of about 300,000, we're averaging 50 to 60 inquiries a week. (Of course, once you cut out all the fat, i.e. people who are not eligible for our program, we're left with only a few worthy candidates. But that's okay; we're looking for quality, not quantity).

In Kamloops we are getting about 40 inquiries a week from our Kijiji and Craigslist advertising combined. We have to do more because the population base that we market to is about 150,000 people.

That's just an example. Depending on where you live and what the population of your area is, your numbers may differ from ours. Do a little bit of research to see which sites get more hits in your area, but don't hesitate to advertise on multiple sites, as long as you target your ads to the right audience.

Where to advertise online?

At the time that we are writing this book, Kijiji.ca and Craigslist.ca are the two BEST online classified websites we've found. However, there are local websites in different cities that are very effective for that particular area. For example, in Victoria, "UsedVictoria.com" may even be more popular than Kijiji and Craigslist.

If you are not familiar with which sites are most popular for your area, just ask around a bit.

For illustration purposes in this book, I'll focus on advertising with Kijiji.ca as it seems to be the most popular, in general, across the country. For example, it works equally well for Dan in Halifax, NS as it does for me in Kamloops, BC.

Here's an example of a typical Rent-to-Own classified advertisement (actually, it's from a competitor of ours in Kamloops):

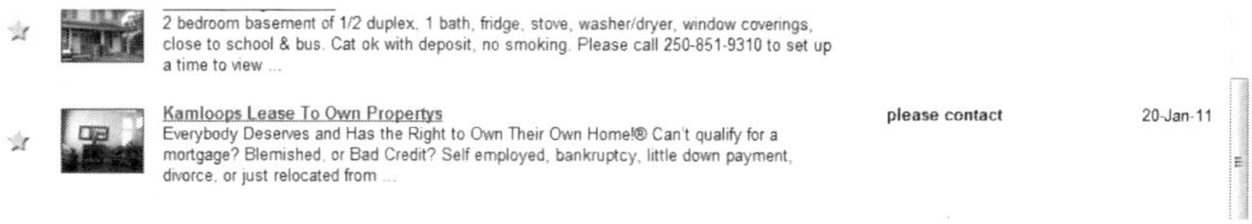

This ad was located in the "Houses for Rent" category. He paid a small fee (which will vary, depending on the size of the market you are in) to have it listed as a "top ad."

Next is an example of the same ad when you click on it and expand it:

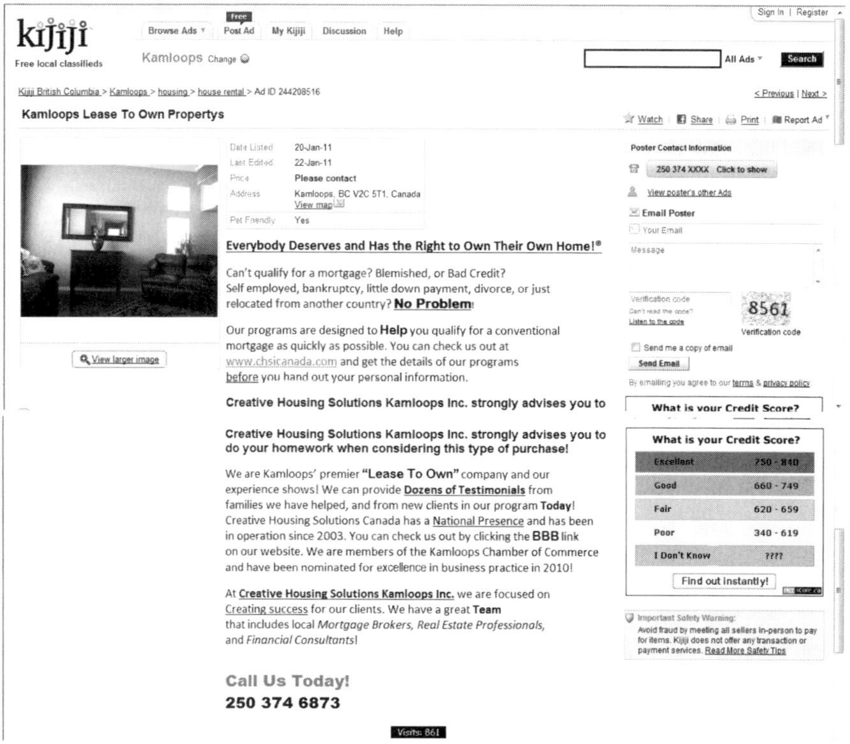

In this case, they suggest that people check out their website first, but then they ask them to "Call Us Today!"

They will get lots of calls and they will waste a lot of time on the phone with unqualified prospects. Of course, that's their choice.

In our case, I don't even want prospects to call us unless they have checked out the website already, and hopefully filled out an application form. That's called "automatic pre-qualifying."

Tips on Posting Online Ads

Post different ads in a variety of categories: Houses for Rent, Houses for Sale, Real Estate Services.

Include pictures. Even if it is a generic photo like the one in the ad above, pictures get people's attention and make your ad more appealing.

You can post for FREE, but your ads will get bumped down by newer ads very quickly. Experiment with posting some FREE ads, as well as paying for "top ad" positioning for some of them.

Be very clear about what you are offering and what you want the prospective person to do.

R2O Marketing Magnet # 4: Vehicle Signage

Let me start with a story:

I was on a road trip and filling up the tank of my FJ Cruiser at a gas station in Merritt (a small town about 45 minutes from Kamloops). Unbeknownst to me, a lady had noticed me and had found my company's phone number. The next day, she called us, set up an appointment and quickly became a client of BCRent2Buy. She is now happily established in the rent-to-own home with us. That deal, if all goes according to plan, will net us close to $40,000 over the next 24 months.

In this case, the total investment for this particular marketing “tool” was about $200. Yes, at least $40,000 in profit for a measly $200 marketing expenditure. That’s a 200:1 return on investment! How would you like to net $200 profit for every $1 in marketing? You can, and I’ll show you how right now.

I’m talking about turning your vehicle into a rolling billboard, with…

Vehicle Signage! That’s right, simple old signage on your car, van or truck can translate into DEALS and profits for you. If you are super-serious, you can even get a full vehicle wrap. This is absolutely the BEST way to do it, as your car or truck will be impossible to ignore. Full wraps can be quite expensive, but there is the option to finance the wrap for $79 to $99 a month – and that makes a lot of sense.

If you don’t want to do a full wrap, then you can consider doing decals on your windows. That is what I did with my first vehicle because the financed wrap wasn’t available at that time. That can work very well too. Just be sure that the colors contrast enough so that the signage is very easy to see.

The challenge with wraps and decals is that once you put them on, well, they’re really “on”. That means that your family has to put up with driving around with you in a big, rolling “Rent-to-Own” billboard. This can be a little dicey if you have a one-vehicle household and your spouse and kids aren’t crazy about being stared at as they drive. I was lucky, mine are. And if they weren't, they'd have to get used to it FAST.

Another big advantage to having signage on your car is that it makes it super-easy to claim your vehicle for business use. How can Revenue Canada argue that you don't use the car for business purposes if there is promotional signage all over it?

One in-between option is to have magnetic signs made for your vehicle. That way you can put them on and take them off as you see fit. This is what I have right now, as my real estate business is local, and I don't want to be advertising it when I am travelling (which I do a lot). The disadvantage to magnetic signage is that the magnets wear out over time. You should take them off when you wash the vehicle, otherwise they can move around and scratch your paint job. They are easy to steal, and they can fall off on the highway.

Some quick notes about signage

Make sure that people can understand what you are all about FAST. You only have about 2 seconds to grab their attention. Right now, my signs say "Renting Sucks: Rent-to-Own." Be sure to include your website and/or phone number. Short and memorable.

Don't be "cutesy" with your wording. You need to get your main message across FAST and CLEARLY. If you drive like a maniac, you will have to take it down several notches. With signage, you are easy to track down! Stick your business cards around your windows when you park – make it easy for people to pick one up so they can contact you.

Try to park your vehicle in high-visibility locations to get the maximum impact from your advertising. (I saw my car on TV once. They were filming a news story downtown and my car was in the background – signage was very visible).

Always carry lots of business cards, pens, paper and promotional material in your vehicle. You never know when someone might flag you over for more information. By being prepared, you look professional, and you can get and give all the info you need.

Although you probably won't have your phone ringing off the hook from your vehicle signage, it is a great 24-hour sales tool for your rent-to-own real estate investing business. Just getting ONE little deal from your vehicle signage can pay off BIG returns for the cost. Plus, having your vehicle with signage on it shows that you are a serious real estate investor, and you will feel like one too.

Other Marketing Avenues

While Internet advertising is your best bet, that doesn't mean you shouldn't deal with print media at all. Some people do respond better to newspapers than the Internet (some folks still believe that the Internet will never catch on!). As for us, in addition to Kijiji, Craigslist and other sites, we also advertise in as many local real estate publications as we can because many people looking for homes are reading them.

Then, there are also tear-tab signs that you put in supermarkets, convenience stores, pubs, restaurants, etc. around your area. One of the tricks of the game is to tear off one tab on the outside and one in the middle, because for some reason people don't like to be the first ones to tear off a tab. But if they see a couple that are already torn off, not only will they tear one off as well, it will show them that other people in your community are also interested in your program. Human nature being what it is, this will make your program even more appealing and desirable.

Another effective way is postcard mailings. Despite what you might have heard about mass mail, it can be quite inexpensive. If you're sending out 1,000 or more cards at a time, you can mail them out as "unaddressed ad mail," which brings your cost and postage at this time to a little over 10 cents for each postcard. You can arrange through Canada Post to send these out to specific neighbourhoods and only to, say, apartment houses where people are tenants, not owners. If you already have a property lined up, you can take a photo, put it on the postcard, and attract people this way. The message it sends is "This is what you could have if you call us."

There are also bus stop signs. One of our competitors is doing very well advertising on mini billboards at bus stops. They're kind of "in-your- face" of a lot of your potential clients. A person we know in Edmonton, Tony Peters, is very successful in the R2O. He actually has huge billboards around the city advertising his rent-to-own business. He's found that to be effective, not just for attracting potential clients, but for also attracting potential investors.

Another thing we've been doing to attract clients is organizing live events, such as seminars about how to become a homeowner. You can promote these for free in the "community events" section of your local newspaper and do the same online with Kijiji and Craigslist. This is also a great opportunity to invite people who have filled out your application, but who have not set up a meeting with you yet. (As an aside, if you are nervous about the idea of doing a presentation in front of a group of people, I highly recommend that you join Toastmasters International. There, you will learn how to speak in public with confidence, while you are practicing in a safe and supportive environment).

There's also social media marketing. You can start up local Facebook and Yahoo groups to promote your rent-to-own business. The pros are that it is very inexpensive to do. The cons are that it can be a huge time-suck and not gain a good return on your precious time.

Last but not least, you definitely want to focus a lot on networking: Getting out there and hob-nobbing with as many people as you can. You want to be networking with mortgage brokers because they can be an excellent source for potential clients for you – just the kind of clients you're looking for (good job, cash, and no conventional mortgage at this time). Also, realtors will be showing houses to different people who haven't been pre-qualified, so they can refer these folks to you.

You can consider joining your local Chamber of Commerce and attending their networking functions. We have found some really good "team" contacts there, as well as potential investors. Rotary clubs and all types of non-profit organizations are also fantastic places to meet “movers and shakers”, and do some good for your community at the same time.

Conclusion

How much you invest in marketing for your rent-to-own business depends on many factors. First, it depends on how much you have to work with, as well as how serious you want to be about the business. The “Top 4” that I shared with you in this chapter can all be set up for $1,000 or less (a lot less if you do your own website). And you can run them for around $150 to $200 per month.

The other consideration is the area where you live. Smaller markets have fewer possible clients and deals; however the marketing costs and the number of competitors should also be lower.

Average profit potential is another consideration. The lower the price of the average “starter” home and the appreciation rate in your area, the lower your profit per deal will be. If your average profit per deal is $40,000, then you should be willing to invest more money into marketing than if your average profit per deal is only $15,000 (which is still pretty good, if you think about it).

Our suggestion is that you start off with the “Top 4” strategies first, and get a deal or two under your belt. Then you should start adding more and more marketing media to your mix as you grow your business.

Bottom line is: You never want to be overly dependant on any one marketing media. Why? Because things can change very quickly and if you have all of your eggs in one marketing basket; it leaves you very vulnerable. In my case, I’m in a relatively small city, Kamloops, so I do a lot of different things to keep my deal flow going:

- ✓ Website
- ✓ Online advertising on Kijiji, Craigslist and in local classified ad sites
- ✓ Classified ads in eight newspapers in and around my city
- ✓ Organic search engine optimization
- ✓ Google pay-per-click advertising.
- ✓ Facebook ads
- ✓ Vehicle signage
- ✓ Tear-tab signs
- ✓ Business cards
- ✓ Networking
- ✓ Live events for potential clients and investors
- ✓ Webinars for potential clients and investors
- ✓ Direct mail
- ✓ Monthly newsletters for potential clients and investors
- ✓ Monthly e-zines for potential clients and investors

And moving ahead I will be testing:

- Regular postcard mailings to renters
- Bus stop signs and billboards
- Radio ads
- TV ads (on cable TV)
- Web TV program
- Regular publicity campaigns

Do you have to get that carried away? No, of course not. I just wanted to show you some of the different marketing and advertising venues that are open to you.

Start small with the "Top 4," and do more as your business becomes more successful and you are ready for it.

Hot Tip: Your Presence in Cyberspace

Having a killer website where potential clients can get detailed information about your R2O program, as well as an online application form, is a good way of running your business. Not sure how to create a website? Hire a web designer / developer on Elance.com, where you can find all kinds of contractors. You can get ideas for a website design and content from our site, www.bcrent2buy.com or from www. atlantichomesolutions.ca

Looking for an inexpensive way to get your own website set up?

Check out Networksolutions.com. It's a one-stop-shop where you can buy your website address (URL), create a good-looking website from the ready-made templates they have, and host it as well.

And if you want, you can hire some local teenager to do it all for you…cheap.

CHAPTER 9

PRE-QUALIFYING CLIENTS

We'd like to start this chapter with a little bit of a warning. The most challenging part of the R2O business is finding the right client to work with. Like any relationship where people have to get along and live in peace and harmony, this can turn out to be a very gratifying experience. However, if you work with the wrong clients, it can turn into a nightmare, and you can lose your shirt in the process. So it goes without saying that finding the right client is crucial. Be prepared to kiss a lot of "frogs" before one turns into a "prince" of a client.

In our own experience, the ratio of frogs to princes is around 20 to 1. This means we have to go through the vetting process with about 20 people before we find one we feel we can work with. It's quite a challenge to find people who don't qualify for a mortgage and yet have a chunk of cash up front, make good money, and whose credit could be fixed enough to buy a house in the next two or three years.

If you're new to this game, you're probably wondering how you sift and sort through these potential candidates. How can you automate as much of this process as possible, so that you're not talking with a whole bunch of people who don't fit your criteria? This is where the Internet is very useful. For us, the biggest prequalification step is to have prospective clients fill out a complete online application form. (We'll give you access to a sample application form we use, and you can create your own from that).

Of course, this means that you'll need to establish a website, which can be done at a relatively low cost (see Hot Tip in Chapter 8). On the website, explain the service you provide: How you're offering to help people get into a home, and that while mortgage lenders are not willing to work with them, you might – if they meet certain conditions.

Explain your program in general terms and invite them to complete the application form, which covers the important points:

- Do they have enough income to support a future mortgage for the home in the price range prevalent in your area?
- Do they have any money saved that could be used toward the option fee in order to make you comfortable enough to go out and buy a home for these people?

In other words, you want to make sure these folks have a good job and income. In our case, we're looking for at least $40,000 in gross family income a year (before taxes). It doesn't just have to be income from their job. It can be all sorts of revenue from within the family group: Child tax benefits, employment insurance, disability incomes or long-term work compensation benefits - revenues from a variety of sources as well as direct employment.

Wherever the income comes from (assuming it comes from legal sources), it must cover all the above-mentioned costs, and be enough for the client to qualify for a suitable mortgage in a couple of years. We talked about a 6% non-refundable option fee. If you're in an area where house prices are higher than average, you may want to be a bit flexible, say 4 or 5%. It's up to you. You should feel comfortable with what you're getting, but don't get into the habit of lowering your parameters too much and jumping on the first person who comes through your door. True, the vetting process might be long-drawn, but it's worth your while to be thorough. We mentioned the 20:1 rule; you might get luckier or you might have to turn over many more stones.

We mentioned that an application form is the first step in your sifting and sorting process. The second is talking to people whose applications sound promising. That's when you get a good idea of who these folks are, what expectations they have, how serious and committed they are about being homeowners, and, basically, whether or not they fit your criteria. It's also a good opportunity to explain to them once more (in addition to what they have already read on your website) about how the R2O program works; dispel any misconceptions they may have so they know exactly what they're getting into – their rights as well as their obligations.

For example, people must recognize that they won't be able to become homeowners for the same amount that they're currently spending on rent. You can say to them, "You're spending $1,500 a month on rent and you'd like us to put you in a $250,000 home, which is $2,000 a month under our program. Is that something that you'd be willing to pay toward a home that will eventually be yours, rather than paying for an apartment you're currently renting?" You should explain it to them plain and simple. To some people, a R2O program might sound fantastic on paper, but once they realize what's involved, and what their obligations are, they're not as enthused.

You can do this initial pre-selection over the telephone. You don't want to set up meetings with all these people right away. Your goal is to assess them fairly quickly on the phone because you will go through a lot of these calls before you whittle down the crowd to a few "finalists".

We said this before, but it can't be stressed enough: Be thorough. Have a list of questions written down so you don't forget anything. Jot all their answers down because at the end of the day Candidate A will blend into Candidate B and you won't know who's who – that's what happens when you interview a lot of people. The questions should include:

- What is their income
- Their credit history.
- The amount of debt they're carrying right now, if any. (New Canadians might very well have a clean slate).

If a candidate sounds like a good prospective client for you (having been informed about all the details of the R2O arrangement so he knows what his obligations are), then you can meet him in person. Ask him to bring his credit report, including credit score.

This can be done online. We prefer to use Equifax (www.equifax.ca) because that is the credit service that most mortgage companies work with. There's also TransUnion (www.transunion.ca). Everyone should be checking their own credit once in a while. It only costs around $25. They get it for free if they ask for it in writing, but it will take 10 days to two weeks to arrive.

That step is another pre-qualifier because if someone is not willing to show you his credit report, chances are he is not all that great to work with. You (or your investors) are putting money on the line and you have every right to ask a potential client for the credit score. If he is secretive about his finances, you should let him go FAST.

Aside from the credit report, the candidate should also bring confirmation of his income: Pay stubs, notices of assessment from the previous year's tax return, or at least a copy of his current tax return or other sources of revenue so that you can see in black and white that he earns at least $40,000 a year. You do need that guarantee because, in essence, you're providing alternative financing to him, so you need proof that he is good for his money. You also want confirmation of his credit standing, allowing you to determine what kind of credit repair plan he is going to need.

Establish to your satisfaction that the candidate has enough family income, his credit score and credit situation will allow him to obtain a mortgage in the next two to three years, and he has money for an option fee.

It's not good enough to say that his aunt Mary might lend him the money. You want to see some form of RSP statement or a bank statement indicating that he has that money accessible to him right away.

Once all of that is in order, ask him to pay at least a $500 non-refundable application fee that will be used towards his option fee to show that he's serious about moving ahead. When that is done, you can hook him up with your real estate agent and let them go shopping for a home.

As for us, we often skip the application fee and just get the entire option fee right up front before we even start the process of letting a client look for a house. However, there's no reason why you shouldn't charge a $500 application fee up front first.

Just to give you an idea of the numbers we're getting when we advertise for clients: Typically, we receive 50 to 60 inquiries a week; out of that, 15 to 20 applications are filled out. We'll whittle it down to between five and seven and invite them for a meeting. At the end, we'll be left with maybe one person every other week who is serious enough to actually give us an application fee or an option fee. That's a lot of filtering. It's like a funnel: A lot of people at the top, but very few make it to the end.

So the thing to learn from our experience is to be very selective. Don't schedule a meeting with every person who shows even a fleeting interest in your program because you'll be wasting your time. Meet only with those whose candidacy looks promising, based on their full understanding of the program, as well as their income, credit situation, and willingness to come up with application and option fees upfront.

Hot Tip: Have a check list ready

Finding just the right candidate for your Rent-to-Own program is going to be a time-consuming process. As explained above, there are several steps to this process. The telephone conversation with the people whom you have selected based on their online application is a very important step because it gives you a better idea of whether this person has the full grasp of the program, as well as financial means to live up to his end of the contract.

Therefore, before you start interviewing the candidate on the phone, have a check list ready with all the things to be discussed and questions to ask so you can stay on track. You should certainly, at the very least, cover such topics as his income, credit history, availability of cash for the upfront payment, and the amount of debt he is carrying right now. Write down all the answers so you can later compare them with those of other candidates. Don't rely on your memory – the more people you interview, the more difficult it will be to remember who's who. But if you have a list of essential points and everything is written down, you'll have a good record of your conversation and will be able to decide whether to invite this particular person for a follow-up, face-to-face interview.

Resource: Get a free copy of the BCRent2Buy checklist at www.RentToOwnProfits.com/Checklist

CHAPTER 10

CREDIT SCORES & CREDIT SCARES

This chapter was written by Wagner Cardozo and Linda Rose-Yelich from Dave Dubeau's company, BCRent2Buy.

Wagner has completed his training to become a mortgage broker, and he works with our clients to help fix their credit and qualify them for a traditional mortgage. Linda has over 20 years of experience in the banking industry and she is a client service specialist. Part of her job is to pre-qualify our prospective clients to make sure they are a good "fit" for our program.

We have dedicated an entire chapter to credit issues and pre-qualifying clients because getting this RIGHT is the back-bone of the rent-to-own business model.

It's easy to find people who want to do a rent-to-own deal. It's NOT so easy to find people who have the income, the cash for a deposit and a "fixable" enough credit to be able to qualify for a traditional mortgage within 2 to3 years.

Again, our goal is to make sure that our clients SUCCEED with us and our R2O program. We don't want them to put in all the money and effort involved, only to see their dream of home ownership go down the drain. And from our point of view, we don't want to go out and buy a house for someone that fits their needs and their tastes, and then have to try to rent-to-own it to someone else who may not have the same tastes.

By properly understanding the prospective client's current credit situation, you will be able to go into the deal with a very clear picture of what needs to happen in order for them to eventually qualify for a mortgage.

So let's find out about credit scores, credit reports and how to work with them. Take it away Linda and Wagner!

What is the importance of the Credit Report and Score?

The credit report and credit score represent the credit worthiness of an individual, in this case being the potential tenant (buyer) – whom we'll refer to throughout this chapter as merely the "tenant". Reviewing the credit report and knowing the credit score are important parts of your due diligence process. Both credit report and credit score are necessary for your evaluation of a prospective tenant.

Lenders use credit scores to determine who qualifies for a loan, at what interest rate and what credit limits. It plays a large part in the bank's decision making process.

As our big picture goal is the tenant's qualification for a mortgage through a traditional financial institution at the end of his term, it is wise to view and understand this document prior to entering into the rent-to-own agreement.

It will give you two key pieces of information to make a decision about moving forward with this potential tenant. It will give you a history of his credit patterns, as well as an indication of the length of time needed to repair the credit to bank lending standards.

It will answer the questions of "Can HE do it?" and "Do you WANT to do it?"

Understanding Credit: A snapshot of financial life & health

Both credit score and credit report can be obtained from the credit-reporting bureaus together or separately.

The CREDIT SCORE is reported as a numerical expression with a range between 300 and 900 – 300 being POOR and 900 being EXCELLENT. A score between 700 and 750 is the goal to aim for at the end of the term with the tenant. A higher score translates into a lower perceived risk for the lender. A credit score is a judgment about the individual's financial health, at a specific point in time.

The CREDIT REPORT is the story/history of the individual's financial life. (It is important to note that derogatory items such as bankruptcy, credit consolidation, and late payments fall off after seven years).

What's in a Credit Report?

- Identifying Information:
  Name, address, Social Insurance Number, date of birth, and employment information are all used to identify an individual. Updates to this information come from information he supplied to lenders.

- Trade Lines:
  These are the individual's credit accounts. Lenders report on each account he has established with them. They report the type of account (bankcard, auto loan, mortgage, etc), the date the account was opened, the credit limit or loan amount, the account balance and payment history.

- Credit Inquiries:
  When an individual applies for a loan, he authorizes his lender to ask for a copy of his credit report. This is how inquiries appear on his credit report. The inquiries section contains a list of everyone who accessed his credit report within the last two years. The report lists both "voluntary" inquiries, caused by his requests for credit, and "involuntary" inquires, such as when lenders order a report so as to offer pre-approved credit in the mail.

- Public Record and Collection Items:
  Credit reporting agencies also receive public record information from provincial courts, and information on overdue debt from collection agencies. Public record infor-

mation includes bankruptcies, foreclosures, suits, wage attachments, liens and judgments.

What's not included in a Credit Report:

- Race, colour, religion, national origin, sex and marital status.
- Age.
- Salary, occupation, title, employer, date employed and/or employment history.
- Where the individual lives.
- Any interest rate being charged on a particular credit card or other account.
- Any items reported as child/family support obligations or rental agreements.
- Certain types of inquiries (requests for his credit report).
- Any information that is not proven to be predictive of future credit performance.
- Whether or not he is participating in a credit counselling of any kind.

Where does the tenant obtain a credit report?

It's a good idea for the tenant to request a copy of his credit report from the two credit-reporting agencies at least once a year to verify that his personal information is up to date, that his financial information is correct, and to ensure that he has not been the victim of identity fraud.

A credit report can be ordered by phone, fax or e-mail. The easiest and safest methods are by mail or online. The credit score can only be ordered online. Although both can be ordered separately, it is more cost-effective to order them together, as when the credit score is ordered, it is accompanied by an online copy of the credit report.

By mail:

The tenant can print out the credit report form directly from the credit-reporting agencies' websites. It can be completed and sent in by mail. The agencies will then provide the tenant, by mail, with a free copy of his report, which he can receive any number of times a year as long as it is requested in writing. Note that he will not receive a copy of his credit score.

By Internet:

The credit report and/or credit score can also be ordered through the reporting agencies' websites. The tenant will receive his credit report online only a few minutes after he has made the request. Credit-reporting agencies, however, charge a fee for providing an online copy of the credit report and/or credit score. There are also several options to choose from. There can be a one time fee for a single request or a monthly charge with unlimited access to the report and score.

The credit-reporting agencies in Canada are:

Equifax Canada
National Consumer Relations
P.O. box 190, Station Jean-Talon,
Montreal, Quebec H1S 2Z2
Tel. (toll-free): 1-800-465-7166
Fax: 514-355-8502
Web site: www.equifax.ca

TransUnion Canada
All provinces except Quebec:
Consumer Relations Centre
P.O. Box 338, LCD 1
Hamilton, Ontario L8L 7W2
Tel. (toll-free): 1-866-525-0262
Fax: 905-527-0401
Web site: www.transunion.ca

When we start working with a client, we ask him to pull his own credit report. We like our clients to be involved in the process of understanding and repairing their credit. When they pull their own report there is no derogatory hit on their bureau, and the reports that they receive are in layman's language with much of the coding used for reporting to professional organizations dropped.

Use the information that you have on the credit report to ask questions of the potential tenants. Why were they late with the payments at a certain time? How did that situation come about? How did they resolve it?

It is important to note that the credit score changes over time and it is vital to monitor and improve this score with the tenant so that he is in a position to purchase his home at the end of the agreement. We recommend that you meet with the tenant on a quarterly basis to go over his credit report and score.

How to read/interpret credit report and score

Credit inquiries are requests by a "legitimate business" to check an individual's credit. As far as the credit score is concerned, credit inquiries are classified as either “hard inquiries” or “soft inquiries” – only hard inquiries have an effect on the credit score.

Soft inquiries are all credit inquiries where an individual’s credit is NOT being reviewed by a prospective lender. These include inquiries where he is checking his own credit score, credit checks made by businesses to offer him goods or services (such as promotional offers by credit card companies), or inquiries made by businesses with whom he already has a credit account.

Hard inquiries are inquiries where a potential lender is reviewing an individual’s credit because he has applied for credit with them. These include application for an auto loan, mortgage or credit card. Each of these types of credit checks count as a single inquiry. One exception occurs when he is “rate shopping”. That's a smart thing to do, and his Equifax score considers all inquiries within a 2-week period for an auto or mortgage as a single inquiry.

The Credit Bureaus do a good job of distinguishing between a search for many new credit accounts and rate shopping for one new account.

Letters, Numbers and Codes

The lenders rate each of the individual’s credit history items. The Credit Bureaus report each item on a scale of 1 to 9.

A rating of “1” means the individual pays his bills within 30 days of the due date. The higher the number, the longer he takes to pay his bills. A rating of “9” means that he never pays his bills, or that he has made a consumer debt repayment proposal to the lender, or declared bankruptcy. There may be judgments and liens.

A letter will also appear in front of the number: for example, I2, O2 or R2. The letter stands for the type of credit he is using.

I: He was given credit on an instalment basis, such as for a car loan, where he borrowed money once and repays it in fixed amounts, on a regular basis, for a specific period of time until the loan is paid off.

O: He has open credit such as a line of credit, where he borrows money as needed, up to a certain limit and the total balance is due at the end of a certain period.

R: He has "revolving" credit, where he makes regular payments in varying amounts depending on the balance of his account, and can then borrow more money up to his credit limit. Credit cards are a prime example of revolving credit.

Helpful abbreviations when reading Credit Reports:

BK: Bankruptcy
BT: Balance Transfer
CA: Collection Agency
CBR: Credit Bureau Report
CC: Credit Card
CCC: Credit Card Company
CCCS: Consumer Credit Counseling Services
CFL: Consumer Finance Loan
CL: Credit Limit
CO: Charge Off
CRA: Credit Reporting Agency (TransUnion, Equifax)
Derog: Derogatory
DMP: Debt Management Program

DOFD: Date of First Delinquency
DOLA: Date of Last Activity
EQ (also EFX): Equifax
EX (also EXP, XPN): Experian
FA: Fraud Alert
FC: Foreclosure
HELOC: Home Equity Line of Credit
IIB: Included in Bankruptcy
INQ: Inquiry
LOC: Line of Credit
LTV: Loan to Value
OC: Original Collector or Original Creditor
PIF: Pay in Full
PL: Personal Loan
PR: Public Record
RECON: Reconsideration
SOL: Statute of limitations
TD: Turned Down
TL: Tradeline (An entry in your credit history)
TU: TransUnion
WO: Write Off

How long will it take to repair the credit score?

Generally speaking, as all situations are unique, a credit score that is in the low 500s will take approximately three years to repair. In the mid 500s to low 600s, it will take approximately two years. When the score is in the mid 600s, it may only take one year to repair. Your aim is to help your tenant improve his credit score to 750 or higher.

How to improve the tenant's credit score

It's important to note that raising a credit score is similar to losing weight: It takes time and there is no quick fix. In fact, quick-fix efforts can backfire. The best advice is to manage credit responsibly over time.

Five factors affect a credit score.

1. Payment history

The payment history affects 35% of a credit score. This includes late payments, consumer proposal etc. Keeping the bills on track is the best strategy to maintain it under control. Three points are analyzed to determine this percentage:

- Recency shows how recently the tenant missed a payment and how long he spent to solve it. This point will have a negative impact on the credit score.
- Frequency shows if a late payment just happened once or if that is a pattern that is "normal" in the tenant's history. Lenders will avoid this kind of person.
- Severity shows how big the problem is. For example, a late payment in the previous 30 days is more severe than that one that happened 120 days ago.

2. How much the tenant owes

How much the tenant owes in such things as credit cards and loans affects 30% of his credit score. It is based on how much he owes in all his accounts together as well as separately. For example, when he has 2 credit cards close to their limits, the best strategy is to lower both together instead of cleaning one first and leaving the other one at a high balance.

The strategy to maximize the limit and pay it off is not the best one. Lenders can report the balance monthly or quarterly, and if the date he made his payment does not coincide with the date the lender reported it, the balance before he paid can affect the score.

It is very important to create a budget and educate the client. Many people have to be taught that a credit card is not "free" money!

3. How long the tenant has had credit

15% of a credit score is related to how long he has been establishing his credit. Lenders expect a minimum of 2 years with good credit behaviour/patterns. Two areas are considered here: The age of the oldest account and the average of all the accounts he has.

A common error many people make in an effort to clean up their credit is to cancel important mature accounts while keeping the new ones. Sometimes they cancel all of their credit cards. This decision can lower their credit score by fifteen percent.

4. His last application for credit

If the tenant is a "credit hunter" or "credit finder" – someone who applies for credit for that free t-shirt or for no apparent reason – he probably has many hits on his report and those hits can affect his credit score by 10%. In this case, education is the key.

Four points are considered here: How many accounts he has applied for recently; how many accounts he has opened; how long has it been since he applied for the last account; and how long the account has been opened.

5. Types of credit he uses

We round up the last 10% with the kind of credit he uses. Many users think they should have various credit accounts such as auto loans, credit cards and department store cards. This is simply not true. Two credit cards are enough to rebuild a person's credit and keep their score growing.

Credit repair strategies

To rebuild the tenant's credit in 2 or 3 years, some strategies are needed to help him be financially prepared to afford a mortgage at the end of the term. Here is a list of some easy things to do to achieve this goal:

1. Get a secured credit card

This is a good place to start if the tenant does not have a credit card or if he cancelled those he had before. He should use the secured credit card for a minimum of 6 months showing good behaviour – paying more than the minimum payment each month and keeping the balance under 50%. Then apply for an unsecured credit card. After he receives these two cards, it is not necessary to look for more credit to build a better score. It is common to see people applying for more credit to buy a car or to get an extra credit card without any real need. He will be tagged as a credit finder or credit hunter. This will reflect badly on his credit score.

2. Set up automatic bill payments

As mentioned earlier, late payments affect the credit score substantially. It is recommended that the tenant set up automatic bill payments with a bank or credit union as it removes the worry of missing or late payments, especially if he has multiple types of credit such as car loans, credit cards, lines of credit, etc. This strategy is very important in the process of re-building credit.

3. Revolving credit

A credit card is a revolving account. This means the payment amounts can vary. Many people think that to improve their credit, they should not use a credit card anymore. This is not true. The user should show restraint in their credit behaviour and keep their balance under control. A good practice is to keep the balance under 50% and always pay more than the minimum payment.

4. Check credit score regularly

By pulling his credit report himself, the tenant avoids negative hits. This is a good strategy for someone planning to rebuild his credit. The tenant can watch changes in the report and follow the score increasing systematically when he uses the strategies to rebuild and improve his credit correctly.

5. Protect his SIN

After obtaining two credit cards, which is enough to show that the tenant is a credit user, he must not give out his Social Insurance Number or any other information about himself. He wants to avoid anyone doing a credit check, and ultimately, showing up as hits to his credit report.

When you are in the final process of getting the tenant qualified for a mortgage, he should use a good mortgage broker to avoid multiple unnecessary hits on his report. The broker will only pull his credit once (therefore causing only one hit). The broker will shop around and find the best rates for the tenant without his credit score taking a beating.

6. Fix mistakes

After he receives his credit report, he should check for errors. Many creditors are fast to report a late payment but very slow to report accounts paid. He should contact the credit company and ask them to fix any errors he finds. Keep receipts of any payments that were made to report and repair the error directly with the bureau if necessary.

7. Negotiate lower payments – accounts in collections

If he has accounts in collection, the best strategy is to negotiate the balance owing to a lower amount. He can also negotiate a lower interest rate.

Red Flags

We have already talked about some things that can affect or damage a credit score. Here are a few more things to look for in choosing your candidate.

1. Consumer behaviour

A credit score is not the final decision when you are evaluating a potential tenant, but it plays a large part. Poor past decisions can affect a person's credit for a long time, even if he may now be completely different in his credit habits. Carefully read and examine the credit report and interview the candidate to check his consumer behaviour. You should also check the knowledge he has in relation to how his decisions affect his credit history and how those glitches appeared in his reports. But the final decision is yours. It will depend on your expertise and your feelings about your candidate.

2. Late or lack of payments

An important area to check on a potential tenant's report is late payments or lack of payments. For many candidates, their credit history is not a priority. If they have failed in their payments without a valid reason, they will probably fail again. This time it will be with you and your monthly rent.

Late or lack of payments can be justified by health problems where their only option was to pay the credit card or to pay for treatment or living expenses. Again, a face to face interview to discuss these things is the key to making your final decision about working with the person or not.

3. Consumer proposal and Bankruptcy

Consumer proposal and bankruptcy are certainly our biggest red flags. If the potential tenant has been through a bankruptcy, in order to qualify for a mortgage, he will need to show PERFECT consumer and credit behaviour consistently for 2 full years after the bankruptcy has been discharged.

If he is in active bankruptcy, but it will be discharged in a few months, you can offer a 3-year plan to give him enough time to rebuild his credit.

It is important to remember that to the banks and lenders, a consumer proposal and bankruptcy are considered the same. If your candidate has already declared multiple bankruptcies or credit proposals, there is no way that CMHC will insure a mortgage for him. Unless you have some good private lenders, or the client has a LOT of money to put towards the home (i.e. up to 30% of the cost of the home), you should decline this candidate.

Monitor your tenant

After approving and moving forward with your tenant, you should monitor him with regular Credit Repair Meetings. We recommend doing this every 3 to 4 months. Prior to each meeting, the tenant should send you his current credit report and score.

When you monitor the tenant, you are showing how important and serious his credit is. Show him how he can improve his score throughout his term with you by following the credit repair strategies.

When you receive his credit report and score prior to each meeting, review them to ensure that he is really working to rebuild his credit. After the meeting, include the "homework" to be completed before the next meeting.

Conclusion

The better you pre-qualify your potential tenant and the closer you work with him during his rent-to-own term with you, the more likely he will be qualified for a mortgage.

The better educated you are about how credit scores and reports work, the better you will be able to help the tenant.

The least you need to be able to do is to determine whether a potential tenant is a "go" or "no-go" for a deal. If you work closely with one mortgage broker, he will probably be willing to provide some basic credit-counselling for the tenant (provided he gets to do the mortgage work for your deals). Just be sure that you are kept up to speed of how things are going so that you don't get "surprised" along the way.

CHAPTER 11

POWERS OF JV'S: WORKING WITH "MONEY-PARTNERS"

Why are we dedicating an entire chapter to working with investors? Because after you've done a few deals, chances are you'll run out of the 20% down payment money. If you want to take this business to the next level, you'll have to start working with other people's money. By then (having done a deal or two yourself), you'll have sufficient experience and infrastructure in place (a website, online application form etc.) to attract investors. The way it works is that you bring your expertise and infrastructure to the table and the investors put up the money, and you both share in the profits.

Generally, your investor is a silent partner. He brings in all the money and you do all the work in terms of finding the client, identifying the property, doing the paperwork, etc. After all that is done, the investor purchases the property on a joint venture basis. This means that he will share all the profits with you, the Rent-to-Own specialist. There are many different ways to set that up. It can be done on a "share the risk" or "share the benefit" basis, or other ways.

Before we look at that, let's talk a little bit about investors and why they would want to partner with you in a R2O deal.

Many people want to invest in real estate, but they are too nervous to do it themselves. They love the idea of having a solid investment that, unlike stocks, bonds and mutual funds, is safe, gives them a good return on investment (ROI), and is hands-off.

Traditional real estate investing scares them because of the ill-reputed “toilet and tenant” hassles, as well as the long-term, uncertain nature of traditional “buy and hold” real estate investing.

If you can offer them a hassle-free, hands-off, no “tenants and toilets” real estate investment opportunity, (which is the Client First R2O program), that is VERY attractive to a lot of folks.

A lot of people realize what a lucrative business this is and they’re very keen to get involved in R2O real estate investing. However, they don’t have the know-how or the time to do it themselves. As you know by now, having read all the chapters, Rent-to-Own real estate investing is not a complete slam-dunk. There’s a lot of work involved in finding and pre-qualifying clients, selecting the property, purchasing it, and running the whole operation from A to Z. So if someone has the money but not necessarily the ability, time or desire to manage the program, partnering with you, the expert, is a really attractive option.

Now, keep in mind that you being perceived as the “expert” is the operative word here, which is why we’ve been suggesting throughout this book that you do a couple of deals yourself before looking for investors. Also, it’s very important that you develop an infrastructure that’s required for a Rent-to-Own deal: You have to create a website and an online application form, as well as the dream / power team. In other words, you have to be in a position to show your investors that you have everything in place and ready to go.

You're saying to the investor, "Look, I have no money of my own in this deal, but I am bringing in other assets, such as my expertise and infrastructure. So you don't have to worry about a thing. Just sit there and wait two or three years for the payout."

With this kind of approach, there's absolutely no reason why you can't get an investor on board to put up all the money required for a deal. We're going to talk about the way we work with our investors and suggest that you do the same thing because we found it to be quite effective.

But first, who are the best investors for your R2O program?

Prime examples of potential investors are **retirees** who have quite a bit of cash put away but don't want the hassle of dealing with mortgage brokers, lawyers, real estate agents, home inspectors, and clients.

"Newbie" real estate investors are another prime group to approach. These are folks who are just getting involved in investing, and they want to take little baby steps before they jump right in. Your program allows them to do this, while learning the ropes from you.

Non-real estate investors who are tired of the roller-coaster ride of the stock market. These are folks who have traditionally invested in either mutual funds or stocks, but have become tired of the volatility of the market. They are looking for a more stable, solid investment – and real estate fits the bill for them. However, they do not want to spend time or expend very much effort on their investment, so they would prefer to be hands-off. Our program works beautifully for them – getting them returns they long for, but have rarely (if ever) seen in the markets.

Even **past real estate investors** who have been through this process, and know how much work it entails, like the idea of putting up the money and letting someone else deal with the headaches. You also have business owners and professionals who are making pretty good money and would like to invest in a safe and profitable venture, but don't have the time to look for deals themselves. All this is to say that there are plenty of people who have deep pockets and would like to be silent partners in a R2O real estate business.

You know these people are out there, but how do you connect with them?

First, there are a few things to take into account. There's a saying that someone who's in grade four looks like God to a kid in the third grade. The same is true in real estate investing. Even if you've only done one or two Rent-to-Own deals (or real estate deals in general), compared to someone who hasn't done any at all, you look like an expert because you already have some experience under your belt. The investors want to come along for the ride with you.

As we already mentioned at the beginning of this book when we talked about how real estate investing provides more security, it's a lot more attractive to many people than other, more risky options.

Unless you know some people personally, finding an investor willing to work with you may take some time and effort. In Canada, each province has its own securities commission, and the rules for offering stocks, bonds, and other investment opportunities are quite strict. In general, you can't just put out a blanket advertising offering unregulated, unsubstantiated returns. You're free to enter into one-on-one partnerships on real estate deals, but you can't place an ad in the newspaper saying that you're offering X amount of return to investors without getting the approval of the securities commission. If you're placing an ad like that (as people sometimes do), you're breaking the law. Sooner or later, you'll get a call from the securities commission and could possibly be subjected to legal consequences. So you have to be very careful about how you put out the message that you're seeking a partner for a real estate deal.

The best way to circumvent the regulations without breaking any laws is to find someone you know, or someone recommended by family, friends, or business associates – a word of mouth recommendation rather than an advertisement.

Once you have some leads referred to you by people you know and trust, contact these potential investors by mail and explain in the letter what you're doing, what your business is all about, etc. Be detailed, specific, and honest, and offer further clarifications, if needed. Basically, you're trying to get these people to put up their hand and say, "Yes, I'm interested. I would like to find out more about it." So again, putting together a compelling sales letter is a good way to do it.

There are other good ways to entice investors. We put out a regular monthly newsletter for potential investors, which we send out to all our friends and family. The idea is to keep in constant contact with people in your circle, just reminding them about what you're doing and highlighting some of the deals you're working on currently, past deals that have been particularly successful, etc. This newsletter will be a constant reminder of what you do, how well you do it, and how they (or people they know) could benefit as well.

Another thing you can do is send out some information, and then follow up with a phone call to see if the recipients read it and have any questions. You might wonder what works best – post or email. You can use either, but keep in mind that emails might end up in a Spam / Junk mailbox, and not everyone checks those.

Okay, let's say your mail or newsletter caught someone's attention and that person contacted you. What do you do next?

The steps would be similar to what you do when you're pre-qualifying your clients: Ask your mortgage broker to talk to this person and determine whether he is in a position to buy a property. In a sense, you're pre-qualifying a potential investor to see whether he or she meets all your criteria as far as financial standing is concerned.

Once approved, the mortgage broker will tell the potential investor what price range he qualifies for, and get all the paperwork done and ready. Basically, you're getting him set up ahead of time so that once you've got a deal, you can move on it quickly. Or, you might already have a client and a house lined up, so it's in everyone's best interest not to procrastinate.

Before you actually purchase any property (or start looking for clients), you should determine what kind of win-win profit-share arrangement you're getting into. In other words, who's responsible for what, and what kind of money each of you pockets at the end of the deal.

In our case, we choose to accept all the risk regarding the R2O client, the management of the property, as well as the exit strategy. We give our money partner a two or three-year time frame. He knows exactly how much money he is going to put in and how much he'll receive at the end. In our case, we pay as much as 12.65% per year return and our investors just sit back and have the confidence knowing that at the end of the program they're going to get back the money they put in, plus the promised return.

Basically, this is what we tell them, "Okay, Mr. Investor, here's the situation. We found the client. We found the property and have it under contract. We've made an offer on it. What we want to do is sign this property over to you. This way, you're going to become our joint venture partner, the money investor. You're going to buy the property. It's going to be registered in your name, so that's your security. You actually own this home but you don't have to worry about all the hassles and headaches of being a landlord because we're going to lease the property from you. The amount that we're going to pay you for the lease is going to cover your mortgage, insurance, and taxes. All your costs are going to be covered in the amount of monthly lease payment. The lease is going to say that we're also responsible for all of the maintenance on the property, so you have nothing to worry about. At the same time, we're going to sign a contract of purchase and sale with you for two or three years down the road and the price is going to encompass all of the money you've put in up front. Here's how the numbers look for your

$250,000 home: You have to pay approximately $55,000 up front, which you'll get back at the end. Plus, we pay our investors 12.65% compounded over the length of the agreement, so that's going to be taken into account. That adds up to $69,795. That's the total amount that you'll be getting back at the end of the program. In the meantime, we're paying all the bills and taking care of whatever problems might come up with the client or the property. We're taking all of the risk for you. We're going to sublet this property to our client. We're going to charge him more than what we're paying you. That's where some of our profit comes in as well as the rental credits for the client. We're going to charge him a different price at the end than what we're going to be paying you, and again that's where our profit margin comes in. All of this is completely 'hands-off' for you."

It's very important to let your partner know that, while R2O is a very secure investment (safer, in fact, than most other investments), it's not 100% guaranteed. After all, in life there are only two certainties, and that's death and taxes. Even if a client breaks the deal and walks away in the middle of the program, you can turn around and find someone else, while keeping the non-refundable option fee in its entirety. And investors are well covered by the contract, ensuring that you won't take their money and skip town with it. They own the property and have it as security for their investment.

If the investor is smart, he will realize that R2O is a very attractive alternative to other investment options such as savings accounts, GIC's, bonds, stocks and mutual funds, which not only yield low returns right now (certainly nowhere close to the 12.65% interest rate you're giving the investors), but they also fluctuate so much, you don't really know what you'll be getting at the end of the day. If he has the choice between a low-interest, uncertain investment, and one that yields a hefty return and doesn't carry much risk, what do you think he'll choose?

Now, that doesn't mean that investors will part with their money easily. They might have questions and comments, and you should be prepared to address them.

For example, they might want to know why they're putting up all the money, while you're getting a "free" ride. You should let them know in no uncertain terms that while you don't have your own cash on the line, you're not exactly a freeloader. By bringing non-monetary contributions such as your expertise, as well as time and effort needed to manage all aspects of the program, you're allowing the deal to be profitable for the investor, while he or she sits back and has a completely hands-free investment.

At this point, you might remind the investors what exactly you'll be doing to ensure the program's success: Providing the expertise and the infrastructure required for a successful outcome. By taking on this responsibility over the two or three-year period, you're saving them a heap of time, effort, and hassles. That's a significant contribution without which the program would not be possible. Money is important, yes, but without anyone to run the whole operation, it is just that – money.

Most of the time, the program runs smoothly, without any glitches. But sometimes it hits a bump in the road – for instance, the client loses his job, is no longer able to pay rent, and moves out. Will the investor pick up the pieces and find a replacement for that person? Nope, that will be YOUR responsibility. Thankfully, you have a good system in place so you'll just turn around and start the "seek and find" process again, while the investor sits pretty and doesn't lift a finger. And what about all the time necessary to find clients, interview and pre-qualify them, have them look for a house, prepare all the paperwork, make sure everything is going well for two or three years, and then prepare the paperwork again to sell the property to the client? Will the investor do any of that? Again, it's a resounding "NO!" All this is to say that while your contribution to the program doesn't involve money, it is nevertheless significant and, in fact, essential to the success of the whole operation.

Now, what happens in the worst-case scenario? Say you get hit by the proverbial bus and you can't complete the deal. Should your investor be worried about losing his money?

Not at all. You can reassure him by letting him know that he is the actual owner of the property and the client who's living in the house has the contractual obligation to purchase it within a certain time frame, which will happen regardless of whether you're in the picture or not. The investor can either manage the property himself and, at the end of the program, pocket all the profit, or find someone to take your place under the same conditions he had with you. Either way, it's a no-lose situation for the investor.

Now, there's another possible scenario – not exactly as dramatic as the one where you disappear from the picture, but still not what you had hoped for. Let's say your partner invested his money into a $250,000 home. However, the real estate market fizzles rather than sizzles, and the property's value goes down rather than up. Should your investor be worried?

Not really. He'll still get his initial investment back, plus the profit, because the client is under contractual obligation to purchase that property. The payout for the investor may not be as high as he had hoped, but it's still there.

Now, you might come across an investor who asks you why he should work with you when he can do it all by himself? You can tell him that if he has the resources – know-how, experience, time, and infrastructure – to run the program himself, then good luck to him. But make sure he knows exactly what's involved and required to make a success of it. Chances are, once he realizes that he can sit back, do nothing, and still get a great profit at the end without the headaches, he'll be happy to partner with you.

And if the investor has past R2O experience (and therefore knows how much work is involved in the process), he may be even happier to leave it all in someone else's hands while he sits in a deck chair with a glass of Tequila, listening to "Don't worry, be happy".

Having been in the game himself, he knows the hassles first-hand, and he'd much rather leave them to you. So whether your partner is a novice or a seasoned investor, each has a reason to delegate the day-to-day running of the business to you.

Now, let's say that through your networking efforts, you have found an interested potential investor. However, that person doesn't have $55,000 lying around. This is where you can use your real estate and financial expertise to educate him about the power of using the equity in his own home as an investment. He can get what's called a home equity line of credit, a HELOC, and put his equity to work making a very good return on the bank's money, and not his own. We call this an infinite return on investment because at the end of the day, the bank is loaning the investor money based on the security of his house, and he turns around, invests with you, and makes a much higher return.

A HELOC can be prime plus 1 or prime plus ½, which is currently around 3% or so. Like any mortgage, you can lock the term in for two, three, or five years to avoid the risk of interest rates going up in the future. So, they're very flexible and you can set one up to match (or closely match) the term length of your Rent-to-Own program.

Let's say your investor does a HELOC. He's making 12.65% from you while paying out 3% to the bank. He ends up making 9.65% a year on the bank's money! Yes, you heard right: He is making money on the BANK'S money, which is a nice change.

Whether he's looking at 12.65% or 9.65%, where else can he get that kind of return on his investment without worrying about market crashes and such? The answer is: Only through R2O!

Another question you might get from investors is, "Is this RRSP eligible?" No, it's not. You can't use your RRSP money as a down payment on an investment property. There is a way to do it using RRSP money for second mortgages, but that's a little bit beyond the scope of this book.

HOT
RESOURCES

CHAPTER 12

LEGAL DOCUMENTATION NEEDED

Hello, my name is Barry McGuire. My contribution to Dave's fantastic new book is the following: An excerpt from my Focus Workshop entitled Deal-Ready Documents. This is another in the on-going series of Focus Workshops that provide investors with the insider and detailed knowledge to become successful, professional investors.

We call it a Focus Workshop because it is 100% focused on providing you with answers to your specific concerns. You will be given direct answers to your issues. You will get answers to questions you probably don't even know you have.

Our contribution to Dave's book is all about the legal side of Rent-to-Own.

In the legal community, Rent-to-Own is often called a Lease-Option. Why? Essentially, a Rent-to-Own Agreement consists of a Lease (rental agreement) with a tenant, and an Option to buy. Two different contracts, the Lease lets them be a tenant, the Option gives them the right to buy for a determinable price within a fixed time period.

Practically speaking, you can use the terms Rent-to-Own and Lease-Option interchangeably.

So that's the introduction. To summarize, for Rent-to-Own (Lease-Options), we will discuss:

- Goals and goal setting;
- How to instruct and get help from your lawyer;
- Options as part of Rent-to-Own;
- Rent-to-Own combining a Lease and an Option

Goals And Goal Setting Are Essential: How Can You Get Somewhere if You Don't Know Where You Are Going?

Marketing, negotiating, yellow letters, your business of real estate and more are all processes, concepts and structures that you will have to master, and have running smoothly to be the biggest success you can. We do want to discuss and integrate what lets you get to the point of needing documentation. If there's no deal, who needs documents?

As mentioned above, successful deal-making depends on a lot of things. If you don't understand Rent-to-Own (Lease-Option) and you can't explain it, deals will be few and far between.

It's great to understand the deal and explain it, but there's one other absolutely vital requirement that comes between understanding your deal and explaining it to the other party, and the final or "backend" documentation that contains all aspects of your deal.

What is that missing vital step? You have to actually write the deal, and I mean you! Deal documents are the 'front end'.

So, once you have a deal firm enough to be put on paper, you have to be able to actually write that deal. You have to write it in a way that clearly sets out and explains the deal. There can't be holes or what-ifs or missing items. If there are holes and what-ifs, your chances of actually concluding the deal are drastically reduced.

Let's review how real estate deals usually work out in the real world. For almost all deals, the real estate purchase contract or offer as it is commonly referred to, is written up by a realtor. In today's marketplace, and over the last five years, the public has been more comfortable if a realtor is not involved due to the presence of Com-Free and other do-it-yourself companies.

These companies offer very basic services similar to what realtors provide and have really taken some of the mystery, at least in the public's eyes, out of writing up a real estate transaction.

Of course there have always been FSBO deals (for sale by owner). During the boom years of 2004, 2005 and 2006, all sellers had to do was pound a sign in their front lawn and soon they were fielding multiple offers and doing it on their own. Many of you will fit into this FSBO category when you are tracking down sellers with circumstances that are out of the ordinary, where you can make a difference and turn potential disaster into a win-win.

What's missing in this last description? A lawyer. There haven't been any lawyers mentioned. You or the realtors are writing up the deals. In my experience, for normal real estate transactions, I get involved in perhaps one out of a hundred deals. When clients are implementing more creative strategies, I might get asked to comment in 5 out of 100 situations.

Let's get this straight; you have a chance to write the deal and write it properly so you can really increase the chances that it will close the way you want it to close. This is an unbelievable opportunity which, if done properly, makes closing the deal so much simpler. It's one of the rare areas of the law that is transaction oriented with quoted fees rather than open-ended hourly billing.

When a set of real estate instructions comes into a law office and is reviewed, every lawyer's fondest hope is: "Please let all my deals be legible, clearly written and without ambiguity or missing items."

Real estate lawyers generally hate, and are not paid for, delving into unreadable scraps of paper that do not, on any level, provide proper instructions. They just want to get deals in, process them quickly and bill the file. When deals are out of the ordinary (that's how creative strategies appear to the average observer), this kind of deal usually takes more lawyer time.

Usually, the staff opens files, does basic analysis and moves a transaction along to where the lawyer is meeting the client, really without much involvement at all for the lawyer.

Creative strategies, on the other hand, including almost all quick turn deals, require a lawyer's overview. Staff will come along and say, "What the heck is Rent-to-Own (Lease-Option)?" The lawyer has to do his own analysis of the deal, and he is hoping against hope that it will make sense and not give him heartburn.

Conclusion: Learn to write your deals properly and increase your chances of a successful, stress-free, standard legal fee type of closing.

LET'S GET STARTED!

How to instruct and get help from your lawyer

We said it previously and we'll say it again. The typical world of residential real estate lawyers is not set up to assist you with anything that is out of the ordinary. Real estate lawyers want lots of moms and pops buying houses to move into with the kids and a dog. These people get a regular mortgage and buy from other normal sellers. Realtors know how to write these contracts and lenders know how to process them.

Any transaction or deal that is out of the ordinary takes a lawyer out of his quoted fee, transaction-based practice. He now has to look at something he doesn't deal with all the time, examine it and perhaps give an opinion or do research and make modifications. None of this fits with his regular practice.

There are a lot of good residential real estate lawyers. What you need to do is understand how you can help them. It's not that tough; there are a number of simple steps as follows:

1. You have to know what you're talking about.

You can't write up a half-baked deal that you don't understand, that makes no sense to someone else, and then expect your lawyer to turn a lump of coal into a bar of gold. To write the deal, you have to understand the strategy. That means you have to spend time educating yourself about whatever strategy you are working on.

There are lots of avenues you can take to learn your craft. Participate in online forums that discuss your areas of interest. Network and mastermind with other like-minded individuals; discuss with them what's been working and what hasn't. What are the pros and cons; what are the issues? Do some research online to see if there are publications by experts that discuss your strategy. Go to a bookstore or the public library and do some research there. Did you know that many public libraries run a research department that have expert, trained researchers available to the public at a laughably low cost?

Then, you have to practice explaining those deals to the other party and writing those deals in a clear, comprehensible way.

If you have a reasonable amount of real estate experience, for example, let's say you have purchased three or so properties, you already have a great basic foundation for understanding more senior or creative strategies. If you then read this book three or four times and, especially, read the contracts and agreements four or five times, you will be well ahead of most other investors.

Read those contracts and agreements with your mind wide open. Think about the clauses and what they mean. Think about what you are trying to accomplish with a particular strategy. Does the contract or agreement help you or hinder you? In most cases, almost every clause in any contract or agreement can be amended or changed to suit your purposes.

Experience will tell you what works best. Did you know that in a room of 100 real estate investors of mixed experience, some with none and some with lots of experience, only about 25% of those investors have read their basic real estate purchase contract – even ONCE!! Don't you be like that. Reading once is not enough. Read it four or five times, make notes and ask questions.

2. Figure out what documents you think you need to implement your Rent-to-Own (Lease-Option) strategy.

Once you have your documents figured out, you can send them along to your lawyer with a cover letter that basically says,

"Dear Lawyer,

I plan to implement a Rent-to-Own (Lease-Option) strategy. Attached are: my basic Lease, Option, and CIAL/CILA letter. I thought it would be worthwhile to send these to you in advance. Once I have a deal, I will send it along."

At this point you can ask your lawyer to review and comment on the documents, or you can ask him how he sees his role in your Rent-to-Own (Lease-Option) strategy. (Be aware that if you ask him to comment and review, there could be a legal bill, as it will take him substantial time to do a proper review and give you an opinion).

Taking this approach makes your lawyer aware that future deals might be coming in from you, what particular strategy you will use and what documentation you expect to implement. He should then comment on how he sees his role. Maybe he expects you to do the Rent-to-Own (Lease-Option) part by yourself. He would get involved only when your tenant exercises the Option.

You can use this approach and format for any of your transactions, modified accordingly. Always follow up with your lawyer to see whether or not he has received your letter and ask if he has any comments.

Remember, unfamiliar or uncomfortable things go to the bottom of anyone's list of things to do (The confused mind says "NO"). Get your letter and paperwork to the lawyer and follow-up quickly to make sure everything is in order. If there is any hesitation on the part of the lawyer or his assistant, or if you're not comfortable, immediately make an appointment. Go in to the office, sit down and go over the deal with the lawyer. Do this as early as you can. Make sure there are no questions or issues.

And that's how to instruct, follow-up and work cooperatively with your real estate lawyer.

Options

Every Rent-to-Own (Lease-Option) includes a form of Option contract. Options are drafted from the perspective of the buyer or the seller. They are mostly referred to as 'options to purchase' so let us start our discussion from that point.

What is it? An option to purchase is a contract between a landowner (often called the 'optionor') and someone who is interested in purchasing or intends to buy a parcel of land, under which the Option Holder (often called the 'optionee') pays the landowner a sum of money in return for the right to purchase the property. It is an offer by the owner to sell, coupled with a promise not to withdraw the offer during the period of the option. Such a contract creates an interest in the landowner's land in favour of the Option Holder and can be registered in the Land Titles Office against the title to the land. It ensures, as its name implies, that the Option Holder will have the option to purchase the land.

Legal basis. An option to purchase is a contract which creates an interest in land in favour of the Option Holder and can be registered against the title of the landowner. In buying an option to purchase land, the Option Holder is not paying for the land but is buying the right to purchase the land. The purchase price for the land is separate from the price of the option to purchase, although the parties may negotiate a purchase price which takes all or some part of the price of the option to purchase into account.

An option to purchase may either specify the purchase price of the land itself, or set out a mechanism for determination of the purchase price.

The landowner's ownership rights to use the land are unaffected by an option to purchase. However, the right to dispose of the property, or an interest in the property, is curtailed. Because the landowner has given the Option Holder a right with respect to all the property, the landowner cannot dispose of part of the property without giving the Option Holder the right to exercise the option to purchase according to the terms of the document.

When the Option Holder exercises the option to purchase, it is converted into a contract for the sale of the land.

How is it created? An option to purchase is created by a written contract between the landowner and the Option Holder, setting out the description of land, the amount payable by the Option Holder for the option, the duration of the option, conditions under which the option may be exercised, and how the option terminates. The option to purchase is then registered in the Land Titles Office so that any other inquiring purchaser will see that the Option Holder has an option to purchase.

How long can it last? Since an option to purchase creates an interest in land, it is subject to the rule against perpetuities. This is a common law rule, the details of which are unnecessary for this book. In essence the rule against perpetuities would limit the term of an option to the life of the option holder plus 21 years. Since most options are for much, much shorter terms, the rule against perpetuities is unlikely to be a factor in drafting your option.

How can you use an option? Controlling a property through an option provides many opportunities including:

1. The basic right to buy a property for your own use;
2. The ability to sell your option to someone else;
3. The ability to combine your option with a lease to a tenant, or
4. Lease to a tenant and sell an option to a 3rd party;
5. The ability to control land while waiting for an event to occur. For example, you might want to change zoning for a property. If you received the zoning change, then you would exercise your option. You might be assembling parcels to do a larger development. Options allow you to control parcels while waiting to see if you can control enough to go forward with development plans.

There are endless variations and applications for options. Options are, as they say in the law, "strictly construed". That means options will be given their plain meaning, So, as with all contracts (but perhaps even more so with option contracts), you must be very careful with your drafting. Beyond the simple options, you <u>absolutely must</u> sit down with your lawyer to discuss what sort of option you want and how that option should be drafted.

Rent-to-Own (Lease-Options)

Our goal today from the legal side is to answer some basic Rent-to-Own (Lease-Option) questions. We will also discuss some of the legal paperwork. First, a brief review of Rent-to-Own (Lease-Option) concepts.

First, if you already own a property, you can Rent-to-Own (Lease-Option) that property to a tenant. Second, and more commonly, the concept of Lease-Option involves you taking control of a new property from the current owner. Your goal in the end, is to sell the property to a buyer you've found, and make some money in the process. You take control from the current owner by leasing their property. At the same time, negotiate an option to buy the property along with the terms of that purchase. Then, you find a tenant to lease the property from you. Along with the lease you negotiate an option for your tenant to buy from you and the terms of that sale.

Important Legal Point # 1:

If someone exercises an option, they are buying a property. You need to have a framework for that purchase. You are investors. How do you usually establish the terms or framework for a purchase? By signing a real estate purchase contract. Most of the Rent-to-Own (Lease-Option) we see do not recognize this point. Would you ever buy a property where the terms are basically, "I might buy this property from you for $200,000 and I've got a year to decide"? That's it, that's your whole contract! What about all the numerous other issues that are dealt with in the standard real estate purchase contract and various schedules you could add? You get the idea.

If the option is exercised, be sure you are in control of the closing process. There are two basic ways to do this. The first way is to just staple to the option a copy of your standard real estate purchase contract. Add a simple clause to your option agreement that says:

"If this option is exercised, it will close according to the attached real estate purchase contract."

You can think about and complete all of the relevant blank spaces in the real estate purchase contract except for the completion date and exactly how the buyer is paying for the property. This is a good approach to take as it allows you to nail down what is coming with the property – what appliances, sheds, real estate property reports – any of those things you would normally deal with in any real estate purchase contract.

If you don't want to attach the actual real estate purchase contract, a slightly less precise approach is to add a clause to your option that says:

"If this option is exercised, it will close according to the most current version of the 'provincial' Real Estate Association contract."

This clause is less precise because you haven't dealt with all those items like appliances and sheds or anything else that you would normally deal with when negotiating real estate purchase contract. But, at least you have a framework.

The third choice is to do nothing regarding the real estate purchase contract. If and when the option is exercised, you then work out the details of the closing.

Important Legal Point # 2:

What legal documents do you need? You can work with your own lawyer to put together a package of documentation for lease options that your lawyer thinks will work and that both you and your lawyer are comfortable with. Dave has some good suggestions.

Our general comments on the legal documents are as follows:

1. The Lease: Every one of you has rented a property at one time, either as a tenant or because you are now an owner and you lease to your own tenants. You are familiar with leases, often called rental agreements. If you like your own lease, use that lease. Or, go to the landlord and tenant section of your provincial service website and use their standard form of lease, modified or not as you see fit. This is really important. Make sure it's a good lease. Your tenant may always be a tenant. He might never exercise the option. Therefore you need a good solid lease to protect yourself as landlord.

2. The Option: Options come in all shapes and sizes. Some are long and some are short but one thing they all must be is, precise. Options are, as the legal cases say, "strictly construed". This means if there's ever an argument, there won't be much legal interpretation by a judge. He will take the plain meaning of the document. If you drafted the option and there is an argument about what a particular clause means, the court will find against you. Make sure your option says what you want to say.

3. The Real Estate Purchase Contract: We spoke about the real estate purchase contract above. Please re-read that section to decide how you want to deal with the question of whether or not to incorporate a real estate purchase contract as part of your Rent-to-Own (Lease-Option) package.

4. Certificate of Independent Legal Advice (CILA): Here are a couple of scenarios: Your tenant is in default under the lease and the option is about to expire. You want to evict him. However, because of the boom, the property is up $100,000 in value. The tenant sees "his equity" disappearing. He goes to court and argues that he is a buyer with equity, not a defaulting tenant with an expiring option. Or, your tenant signed the lease option at the height of the boom and paid you $25,000 in option money. The property value has dropped by $100,000, the tenant will never exercise the option and he argues he should get his option money back. In either case you are the bad, old investor taking advantage of the poor tenant. I strongly recommend you forcing the tenant to see a competent real estate lawyer to have the Rent-to-Own (Lease-Option) explained. Don't close the deal unless there is a CILA where the tenant acknowledges that he is a tenant with an option to purchase not a buyer under some version of a deferred purchase plan. This is very important as the courts treat a buyer very differently than they treat a tenant. Your call on whether you want to get a CILA signed. Of course you won't need it until you're in court. Later in this chapter is an example of a CILA.

5. CILA Letter to Tenant (Buyer): Everyone agrees it's a great idea to make sure your tenant gets independent legal advice.

However, at many of our Focus Workshops where we ask for a show of hands on the question, "Who has actually sent their tenant for independent legal advice," guess what the answer is? Not one! That is why we have developed a letter for our clients to send to their tenant. It states the things that would be included in an actual Certificate of Independent Legal Advice that is signed by a lawyer. The key thing is that you are strongly recommending that the tenant see a lawyer. You are also explaining in simple, easy to understand language that the tenant is a tenant with an option to buy. He is absolutely not a buyer creating equity.

SPECIAL BONUS OFFER:

Email us at donna@barrymcguire.ca for a template of this helpful CILA Letter to Tenant!

Does this letter guarantee success if the tenant goes to court and claims that he is a buyer with equity thus giving him a different characterization and a stronger set of rights? No, it does not guarantee success, but it will certainly be a lot better for you if you can show the court what you sent to the tenant and that they acknowledged they were a tenant not a buyer creating equity.

Rent-to-Own (Lease-Option) Nuggets:

How a Rent-to-Own (Lease-Option) strategy works

Let's review. As one simple example, you sign a lease with the current owner, agree on the Option terms, decide how to deal with the real estate purchase contract issue, and get the Option signed. You don't need the CILA when you are the optionee/tenant. Better to leave it open for you to argue that you are a buyer not a tenant. Now you have a Rent-to-Own (Lease-Option).

When you find a suitable tenant who wants to buy, you start with your lease. Then, you work out the option terms. Again, decide how to deal with the real estate purchase contract issue and decide on whether or not you're going to insist that the tenant get independent legal advice and provide you with that signed CILA. There you go, another Rent-to-Own (Lease-Option).

Your Rent-to-Own (Lease-Option) from the current owner and the Rent-to-Own (Lease-Option) to your tenant are often called a "Sandwich Lease-Option".

Some other issues to learn about and to watch out for are:

- ✓ Make sure you have enough of a 'spread' between the price you can lease-option for from the current owner and, in turn, the price you can lease-option to your buyer for. You need a solid spread on both the price and the rent.
- ✓ Get as much option money up front as you can from your tenant. The statistics say the bigger the option money, the more chance you have your tenant will actually exercise the option and buy from you.
- ✓ An option by you or your tenant is protected by filing a 'caveat' at the Land Titles Office.
- ✓ When negotiating your Rent-to-Own (Lease-Option) with the current owner, you may find that the owner wants to continue to sell or perhaps list the property. You could consider a couple of clauses that you can offer to the seller leaving them room to carry on limited marketing if that's what they want.
- ✓ Remember, full disclosure with a motivated seller is your best key to success. Your seller has to know upfront that you plan to lease and hope to sell the property to a third party. You want the seller to cooperate by doing a simultaneous close with your tenant using one Transfer of Land.
- ✓ Even though mortgages are now assumed less frequently, if the seller wants you to assume his existing mortgage, then your tenant should also be contractually obliged to assume the mortgage. If your tenant decides to get new financing, the seller will most likely have a payout penalty. In order to get their own new mortgage, the seller would have to discharge his existing mortgage and probably incur some prepayment penalties. The seller won't like prepayment penalties. Take this into account in your negotiations.
- ✓ How long (length of time) should the option be? You would like a lengthy option or the right to renew the option for a

number of terms. Probably, the seller wants a shorter option period. It is very important to have a fixed price for the purchase, or, if you don't have a fixed price, a way of determining the purchase price. In a rising market, sellers will not want to commit to a fixed price for a lengthy option period, although you might want that. They will clearly understand that agreeing on a price now for an option that lasts five years could have them selling their property for way less than what it would be worth in five years. On the other hand, if you negotiated your option price at the height of the boom, you as buyer would not be too happy paying boom prices two years after the boom has collapsed. Think carefully about your pricing mechanism and the term of the option.

✓ Combined lease-option or separate lease and separate option? The combined lease-option is okay when you Rent-to-Own (Lease-Option) from current owner. For your tenant, we favour the separate lease and separate option. In court you are always better off if the lease doesn't mention the option. That doesn't mean we think that in a dispute over the lease that the option would not be mentioned. This applies when you are in court to evict a tenant who has defaulted under his lease. In this case you want him to be just a tenant. Separate leases and options are also important if your tenant has gone to court because he isn't able to exercise the option and is frantically trying to save the $100,000 equity he thinks he has built up. You want the judge to see a straight option agreement that has simply not been exercised. NOTE, it is just a fact that courts are sympathetic to and favour the tenant. No matter how good your documentation is, there is always a much better chance the court will find in your tenant's favour.

- ✓ In a dispute, you know the courts favour the tenant. Don't let arguments or disagreements deteriorate so that there is no way to solve a problem except by going to court. Remember the concept of win-win. You can extend options, work out ways to cure the defaults, get further option monies or refund portions of option monies. Find a way to make it work because that is almost always better than going to court.
- ✓ While the lease should not mention the option, the option should say that default under the lease is default under the option.
- ✓ Keep it simple. As mentioned above, we believe that one large payment of option money is the best indicator that your tenant will exercise the option and actually buy the property from you. We don't like leases or options that take a portion of monthly rent and characterize those monthly payments as further option monies. The buyer always wants these extra monies to be included as part of their deposit when they go to see their lender. Lenders don't like this unless they can see that the portion going for rent is actually the market rent. Extra monthly option monies are also often improperly described. The extra monthly monies and the improper description help the tenant argue that he is a buyer not a tenant. Extra payments are also more difficult to administer and keep track of.

Important Legal Point # 3:

This may be the most important legal point of all. Success in a Rent-to-Own (Lease-Option) program is more than the legal paperwork. It is absolutely all about working extremely hard to understand and implement a new strategy. Success in any new program or strategy is a lot of hard work accomplished over a lengthy period of time with lots of ups and downs. It doesn't happen overnight. Malcolm Gladwell, in his best-selling book, *Outliers*, says that the people who are at the very top of their skill and profession take approximately 10,000 hours to get to the top. Don't kid yourself. It takes time to get good at anything and lease-options are no exception.

Once you find a motivated seller or tenant and you negotiate a win-win deal, generally, the legal paperwork follows along nicely. When everyone is happy and the deal is truly a win-win, you can have short options or long options, combined lease-options or separate documentation, get a CILA or not, and it all works out. Yes, you need great legal paperwork. But, you should also be spending lots of your time on the other aspects of your strategy.

Conclusion: The Rent-to-Own (Lease-Option) concept is fundamentally simple. We believe the trick is to understand how the program works, how to find and then negotiate successfully with motivated sellers. If you can find properties with reasonable spreads and motivated sellers, then you should be able to find tenants and complete the loop.

The power of the Caveat

Caveat is the Latin word for 'beware'.

It is the way the Land Titles Office allows registration of "interests in land" that are not registrable on their own. For example, a mortgage is registered against the title as a mortgage. But, the following are not registrable on their own:

- a Joint Venture,
- an option,

- right of first refusal,
- a purchaser's interest in a real estate contract that has not yet closed, and
- most importantly for the purposes of this discussion, an interest in a Joint Venture Agreement purchaser's equitable interest in an AFS.

What to do? All of these 'interests' are registrable by way of a caveat.

The caveat declares the particular interest that someone is claiming, and the caveat is registered against the title. In the case of a Rent-to-Own (Lease-Option) interest, the caveat would state, "I, Joe Investor, claim an interest as beneficial owner pursuant to an Option Agreement in those lands standing in the name of Bill Homeowner and legally described as, (insert legal description)."

Now, your interest in the Option Agreement is registered against the title.

Important Point

The caveat contains the non-title holder's address for service. Any legal action only has to be sent to, not received by, the caveator at the address as listed in the caveat. So, if you change your address you must also change it on the caveat or run the risk of having your caveat and, of course, your protection, disappear without you knowing it.

Cost

You can prepare and file an Option Caveat on your own if you choose. There are certainly some cost savings. Our firm charges $295 +GST. Other firms might charge more or less. Filing on your own could save you at least $250. Are you comfortable doing this? My advice is to leave the lawyering to the lawyers.

What information do I need?

1. a copy of title (to confirm the legal description and EXACT title details)
2. municipal address of the property (so you can cross-check the legal address)
3. name of caveator (person filing the caveat)
4. address of caveator (make it the most permanent address)
5. “interest” claimed pursuant to what? (in this case, as an optionee, pursuant to an Option Agreement)

Please note that Land Titles is very particular about this. Everything must match exactly with the title info, and to their own system checklist. They will, and do, reject Document Registration Requests for what seems like a very small error!

Can I / should I do this myself?

There are serious issues to be considered when deciding to file a Caveat on your own. To name a few:

- claiming the appropriate interest
- filing against the right title
- filing at the appropriate time and in a timely way

- saving money on legal fees versus your peace of mind (your own temperament is a big factor).

Things you should know

Land Titles will send a copy of every Caveat to the registered owner of the property. Caveats have scary words like "I forbid the registration of any person as Transferee or Owner of, or of any instrument affecting that estate or interest, unless the Certificate of Title is expressed to be subject to my claim."

Any owner or seller in an Option deal should be advised that a copy of Caveat might arrive. This always scares them, so make sure they understand that it's part of the process and nothing to worry about.

Independent legal advice

"People are free to take risks and make bad deals," the court says, "as long as they are aware of those risks and the possible adverse consequences."

A Certificate of Independent Legal Advice is a document that confirms that a person has received legal advice on a proposed contract, from an independent lawyer not associated with the other contracting party. This legal advice is meant to make them aware of the risk and possible adverse consequences.

Lawyers often refer to these documents by their acronym: CILA as in "have your client sign a CILA".

Clients often view independent legal advice as a mere formality, and approach the lawyer with an attitude of "let's get this over with quickly". But, the point of these consultations and certificates is to prevent a person from later claiming that he or she didn't realize the consequences of, or even knowing what they were signing.

Your tenant in a Rent-to-Own (Lease-Option) or your Money Partner in a Joint Venture will often resist this step. But really, it is in everyone's best interest to have them do it.

Certificate of Independent Legal Advice

I,________________________, Barrister and Solicitor, do hereby state that I had been consulted by ________________________, the Optionee, with respect to an option agreement ('option') for property municipally described as ____________________________ and legally described as ___________________________________.

I have examined the option, explained to the optionee their rights under the option and further explained and confirmed that the optionee understands they are a tenant with an option to purchase the above described property. I have also advised the optionee specifically that they are not a buyer with equity nor is the optionee creating any equity or any rights other than those as set out in the said option. I further explained to the optionee that any lease agreement and any option agreement individually or collectively are not a real estate purchase contract or any form of purchase agreement.

Dated and signed at______(province)______, __________20___

Barrister & Solicitor: ___________________________________

DON'T FORGET OUR SPECIAL BONUS OFFER:
Email us at donna@barrymcguire.ca for a template of this helpful CILA Letter to Tenant

The Last Word

Here are a few more reminders and repeat items, a few more gems, a few more comments or perspectives that will help you make a success of whatever strategy you employ.

Overall the major item that I think bears repeating is that you need to know your documents. If you can explain convincingly and with confidence your Rent-to-Own (Lease-Option) and how it works, your job is half done. The party you are dealing with won't think you are an idiot. Your lawyer will appreciate the effort you have put into understanding your documents; it makes his job so much easier.

Whatever your strategy, pick the documents you want to use and then get extremely familiar with them. Remember, getting familiar takes reading those documents three to five times. Don't rest until you have all your questions answered and you thoroughly understand every paragraph.

Now, some specific comments:

Options

1. Options have the potential to be amongst the simplest of strategies. All you need are the parties, the property, option consideration, length of option and the purchase price or way of

establishing the purchase price. However, rarely do option situations seem to be as simple as this.

2. The potential to be a simple strategy doesn't mean the actual option situation is simple. Simple or complex, it is very important that you think through all details of your option. Get the details into your option. It will be rare that you continually write the same kind of option. Of all the strategies, it has the most potential to need a brand-new framework every time. It is definitely worthwhile reviewing the option with your lawyer to see whether or not he thinks the details are clear and unambiguous, and is drafted properly.

3. Make sure the optionor (person who sold you the option) knows that the standard way to secure an option is to file a caveat against his title claiming an interest as an optionee pursuant to an option. It's not that you don't trust him or think he will sell the property out from under you or option it to someone else, it's just the way it's done, just business. Remind him that if you do file a caveat, a copy will be sent to the address on the title. The copy of the caveat document that arrives in the mail from the Land Titles Office is at least mildly scary and it's good to remind people and give them that heads-up.

4. Options have an attractive feature that makes them quite different from lease-options, agreements for sale or joint ventures. Options are simple to analyze, and therefore are more saleable.

There is no lease to look at or any real need for a certificate of independent legal advice such as you have with a Rent-to-Own (Lease-Option). Agreements for sale and joint ventures have lengthy documentation and must be looked at from a number of different angles. On the other hand, an option stands on its own. One document gives all the details any buyer of the option needs to know. The filed caveat and copy of title showing the caveat give your option buyer confidence that this is indeed a real deal.

You don't have to ask the optionor's permission to sell the option. They are simple to advertise and simple to explain. "I own the right, for the next year to buy this property for $300,000. Would you like to own that right?" How tough is that? A simple assignment from you to your option buyer is usually sufficient to document the sale.

5. Last point and a very important one. DON'T MISS THE OPTION EXERCISE DATE! Extensions do not have to be granted. If you miss the date and the optionor/ seller does not want to be nice, he doesn't have to. Your option expires, worthless. So find a way to diarise that option exercise date. Record it in your calendar or day-timer or cell phone. Have it pop up as a reminder on your computer. It doesn't matter how you do it, do whatever it takes to make sure you don't miss the all-important option exercise date.

Rent-to-Own (Lease-Option)

1. If options are simple, then a Rent-to-Own (Lease-Option), at least on the surface, is much more complicated. At the minimum, you have at least double the documents, an option and a lease. Suppose your strategy is the "sandwich lease". You find an owner who wants to rent his property and wouldn't mind selling under the right circumstances. You negotiate a Rent-to-Own (Lease-Option). You don't attach a real estate purchase contract but only reference it as the framework for closing if the option is exercised. However the option is for five years so you file your caveat(s) claiming an

interest pursuant to the lease and the option. Both interests are separately caveatable. That's three documents – a lease, an option and the caveat.

2. Having tied up the property with your Rent-to-Own (Lease-Option) from the owner, you now find a tenant and that completes this "sandwich". For the lease option to your tenant, you might include a real estate purchase contract attached as a schedule to the option in order to have certainty around how to close the deal if the option is actually exercised. And again, it's always a good idea to have a certificate of independent legal advice. And now we have an additional four documents if you use a separate lease and a separate option, and three documents if you use a combination lease-option – a lease, an option, the caveat and the CILA – to add to the previous three.

3. My advice is to be careful; eyes wide open with lease options. If an option on its own is relatively simple, but you still need a clear, unambiguous document, how much more difficult it is it to employ the "sandwich lease" strategy where you might need 6 to 8 documents to properly paper all the transactions? It obviously can be done but you should recognize the steepness of the learning curve and the amount of time required to get all these documentation ducks in a row.

4. Under the option section we talked about reminding an owner that you might file a caveat protecting the option. It seems absurd but in a "sandwich lease" situation for a lengthier lease and option, you might see four caveats filed. You file two caveat's, one protecting your lease and the second protecting your option. Your tenant files two caveats regarding his lease and option from you! That would be an interesting title to look at!

5. Consider whether or not instead of the classic "sandwich lease", you might want to try the, "open face sandwich lease" strategy. Many property owners with a property or two and no training consistently under-rent their property. They just have no idea of what rent should be. They pay no attention to market rises in rent. It's much more important to them to have a tenant who is "no trouble" than to get market rent. It's no wonder the tenant is "no trouble". If I were paying 25% less than market rent, I would be no trouble too!

If you are on top of the rental market and know exactly what properties will rent for, and even better if the market is currently strong, you can snap up under-rented properties. Owners who under-rent are often owners who don't like the rental business and regret the day they decided they wanted to be the next Boardwalk. They are often approachable about a Rent-to-Own (Lease-Option) rather than just a straight lease. Get as long an option as you can.

With your lease-option signed and in hand, you go about doing what you do best and rent that property at full market rent to your own tenant. BUT, you don't give your tenant an option and you keep your tenant on six-month leases. You retain the option yourself while keeping an eye on the market. If prices are rising, you can market your option to the world at large instead of having it limited to your tenant. This hugely expands the possibility of making some money on the option side.

BARRY C. MCGUIRE

Lawyer ▪ Author ▪ Teacher

Veteran Real Estate Lawyer

- A lawyer for more than 35 years, Barry's practice has been focused exclusively on real estate for the last 25 years.

Real Estate Investor

- Barry started investing in real estate more than 37 years ago.

Speaker & Educator

- Barry speaks to many groups, including the 3,000+ member Real Estate Investment Network (REIN).
- His popular *"Tales From The Trenches"*, real life stories of investor legal land mines, teaches through example.

Bestselling Author

- Barry is the co-author of *"97 Tips For Canadian Real Estate Investors"*. This book provides insights, strategies and success stories to help you build wealth faster and save time and money.
- All proceeds are donated to Habitat for Humanity.

Teacher

- Barry has self-published an educational newsletter for realtor and lenders.
- He has been extensively involved with the Alberta Real Estate Association in preparing and teaching credit courses for real estate agents.

- The Law Society of Alberta has also enjoyed Barry's help in teaching courses to articling students in the bar admission program.

Barry C. McGuire's Focus Workshops are intensive, one-day seminars that challenge and empower real estate investors to take their business to the next level. Focus Workshops have been presented across Canada.

www.barrymcguire.ca

WRAPPING IT ALL UP...

Well there you have it! Rent-to-Own Profits for Canadians. We hope that you have enjoyed reading this book as much as we enjoyed writing it. More importantly, we hope that you will be inspired to go out and take ACTION on what you have learned here. We highly encourage you to get even more education about creative real estate investing. Join a local real estate investor's group in your area (http://www.creonline.com is a good resource for finding clubs in Canada). If there isn't one, go ahead and start one!

Hang around with other active investors – offer to help them out in exchange for learning from them. Many will be flattered by that. A "free" lunch goes a long way, and can create a mentor for you to turn to when you need assistance.

Start creating a database of potential investors BEFORE you have a deal on the go. Talk to the people you know about what you are up to. Like the old adage says: Dig your well before you are thirsty.

Create you initial "Power Team" – it doesn't have to be perfect from the get go, and you can change as you progress – but you need a team to get started.

Get your legal paper-work together ahead of time. Ask for references for a local lawyer who is familiar with lease-options. If you can't find one locally, look in larger cities in your province. It is worth it to pay a bit more to have the proper documents done, right from the start. Make sure that the lawyer has EXPERIENCE in doing lease-options, and you are not his or her first client with this.

Then start looking for qualified clients! Remember to set up your own systems so that you are not a "slave" to the phone, and you can get people to pre-qualify themselves as much as possible.

Be prepared to screen a lot of people to find the right "match" for you. Don't be tempted to work with really "marginal" clients – as I guarantee you that they will come back to bite you in the butt. Take your time, and put off your first deal until you find the right match (credit poor, cash rich – good job and fixable credit!).

Remember, you can get valuable resources for FREE at www.RentToOwnProfits.com, and feel free to contact Dan Dubeau directly at www.AtlanticHomeSolutions.ca, and Dave Dubeau at www.ResultsHoldings.com

We wish you all the best with your future real estate endeavours.

"I have been impressed with the urgency of doing. Knowing is not enough; we must apply. Being willing is not enough; we must do." Leonardo Da Vinci.

Go out and "do".

Cheers,

Dave Dubeau and Dan Dubeau.